Advertising Media Models

Advertising Media Models

A Practical Guide

Roland T. Rust
University of Texas at Austin

Lexington Books
D.C. Heath and Company/Lexington, Massachusetts/Toronto

Library of Congress Cataloging-in-Publication Data

Rust, Roland T.
Advertising media models.

Includes index.
1. Advertising media planning—Mathematical models.
I. Title.
HF5826.5.R87 1986 659.1'11 84-48438
ISBN 0-669-09375-0 (alk. paper)

Published simultaneously in Canada
Printed in the United States of America
International Standard Book Number: 0-669-09375-0
Library of Congress Catalog Card Number 84-48438

The paper used in this publication meets the minimum requirements of American National Standard for Information Sciences—Permanence of Paper for Printed Library Materials, ANSI Z39.48-1984.

86 87 88 89 90 8 7 6 5 4 3 2 1

Contents

Tables and Figures

Tables

Figures

Preface

In 1973, Dennis Gensch wrote *Advertising Planning: Mathematical Models in Advertising Media Planning* (a work based largely on his dissertation), which was especially useful in establishing several of the features essential to successful media models. This book was followed in 1976 by Jean–Louis Chandon's doctoral dissertation, *A Comparative Study of Media Exposure Models,* which has served as a standard reference to advertising practitioners and academics alike for a decade.

In the ten years that have now elapsed since Chandon's landmark study, there have been many significant advances in the state of the art of media models. Few of the best models of 1976 remain the best today. There is a need, therefore, for a book that catalogs in one place the top media models now available. This book critically reviews the current leading media models, many of which have been published only in the past five years.

It is not possible to evaluate models that have not been made available to public scrutiny. Such models may hold a significant proprietary edge. Or, more likely, they may contain flaws which would prove embarrassing if revealed.

The general level of the discussion is relatively untechnical, although enough equations are included to facilitate implementation. Even an individual with weak mathematical training can probably follow the discussion pretty well by simply skipping over the equations. Most of the book is in plain English.

The book should be a useful reference for media planners, both in industry and in advertising agencies. It should also be helpful as a textbook in graduate courses in advertising media planning or marketing models, and as a reference for media researchers.

There is no claim as to the technical completeness of the book. It would be impractical to include all of the technical details of all the models. It is hoped that the chapter references will be helpful in guiding the reader to further information. In addition, three articles are reprinted in their entirety following the chapters in which they are discussed.

As in any review, there is a certain amount of judgment involved in the evaluation. Some models containing a fatal flaw may appear to be evaluated harshly, even if they reflected an advance at the time of their original publication. Models are reviewed primarily in terms of their current usefulness.

This book makes no pretense of being the last word in media models. The media environment is rapidly changing. Many bright people are busy trying to solve the new problems, while others make attempts at the old problems. No doubt in another ten years, providing we are able to avoid nuclear holocaust in that interval, another author will write a book in which he or she will be able to say that few of the models that were state of the art in 1986 are still the best.

Acknowledgments

Many people have been very helpful to me in this effort. Thanks to Jay Klompmaker and Bob Headen, who got me involved in this subject area in the first place. Thanks to Bob Leone, Mark Alpert, Mary Zimmer, Naras Eechambadi, and the others with whom I have written articles cited here. Thanks to Bill Perreault for his encouragement and advice.

Thanks to my then department chairman, Bob Peterson, who told me to go ahead and write the book but not let my article production slip! Thanks to Caroline McCarley for seeing the promise of this topic and taking a chance on a first-time book author.

Last, but not least, thanks to Pat Stout for being so nice, and for always being in enough of a jam to make me forget my own deadlines.

1
Introduction

The book is organized according to the types of models discussed, and to some degree follows the chronological order in which models of a particular type were developed. First, in this chapter, the media decision process is described. This process is necessarily simplified, but provides the logical framework for the models which follow.

Chapter 2 opens the discussion of specific models, starting with simple models for estimating reach, the total audience of the advertising schedule. The following chapter then describes the models proposed to estimate audience overlap, duplication, of media vehicles.

Chapter 4 begins the examination of the more modern media models, starting with models of frequency distribution of exposure, while chapter 5 provides descriptions of the leading media selection models. Chapter 6 involves recent models for solving some important problems concerning television, including ratings prediction and optimal program scheduling.

To close the book, chapter 7 suggests changes that are likely to be seen in future media models, and their implications for media modeling. Also, because the media area is unusually heavy in jargon content, a glossary is provided to help the reader cope with some of the terminology used to describe the models.

In addition, reprints of three important journal articles follow the chapters in which they are discussed. This is done to retain completeness of presentation, while avoiding overly difficult technical material in the body of the text.

The Media Decision Process

For the most part the models presented here involve decision making from the vantage point of an advertiser, although models of use to television networks are discussed in chapter 7. The assumption is made that an advertiser is wishing to select an advertising schedule made up of particular media buys, such that a specific advertising objective (such as sales or awareness) is achieved to the best extent possible. This almost always involves several steps.

A concise overview of the media-planning process is given by Barban, Cristol, and Kopec.[1] Other useful guides have been written by Jugenheimer and Turk[2] and by Surmanek.[5] More comprehensive texts have been written by McGann and Russell[3] and by Sissors and Surmanek.[4] While invaluable for explaining the differences among media, and the media-planning process, these references fall short of providing a detailed review of media models. This book attempts to fill that gap.

Components of the Media-Planning Process

The media-planning process will be described here as involving four components: operationalization of the overall marketing strategy, creation of the media plan, evaluation of media schedules, and selection of media schedules.

Marketing Strategy and Media Planning

Advertising is part of marketing, which means that the advertising media plan should be consistent with the overall marketing strategy. In addition, the marketing plan typically determines the budget available to the media planner.

The characteristics of the product itself may have implications for the media plan. For example, the product may be intimidating technically (for example, a hand-held camera). In such a case video television may be ideally suited, because the actual operation of the product may be demonstrated.

Distribution also requires coordination between marketing and media planning. It does no good to advertise a product where it is not available. The geographic overlap of the media must be examined carefully to ensure most efficient coverage.

In general the promotion strategy employed may be viewed as being on a continuum from "push" to "pull." In a "push" strategy the thrust of the marketing effort is toward the distribution channel. Trade advertising may be more effective in this case. On the other hand a "pull" strategy is designed to increase consumer demand, and thus indirectly produce pressure on the channel to stock the product. This strategy uses more emphasis on consumer advertising.

An effective sales tool, sales promotion (the use of coupons, in-store displays) is particularly effective when it is coordinated with advertising. This has implications especially for the timing of a media schedule, so that it appears at a time when it will best reinforce a promotion. Similarly, packaging, which may be viewed as a mini-in-store display, may also influence media strategy. An example is the cover of the Wheaties box, which usually features a prominent sports celebrity, who is then featured in television spots showing the star in action.

An important element of the marketing plan is the selection of a target market. This is composed of two parts: the geographic area to be targeted and the group to be targeted within the geographic area. The latter is sometimes called the target group.

There are so many standard sources for analyzing the potential of a market that they will not be listed here. Jugenheimer and Turk provide a good summary of the available data.[2] For our purposes it suffices to say that some products do well in some markets and badly in others. Also competitive advertising can be heavier in some markets than in others, perhaps influencing the budget allocation across markets.

It is useful to target consumers according to their characteristics. Useful typologies are demographics (for example, age and sex) and psychographics (for example, "yuppie"). An attempt can then be made to seek out media with appropriate demographic or psychographic profiles.

The Media Plan

The media plan formalizes the objectives of advertising in the selected media, and produces a concrete, quantified plan for achieving the objectives. Major elements of the media plan are budgeting, developing the media mix, and finalizing the media plan.

Methods of setting an advertising budget are reviewed well by Sissors and Surmanek.[4] Typically the media planner may assume that the advertising media budget is fixed. The budget must then be allocated to particular media, and, within media, to particular media vehicles.

Allocating the budget among the different media involves a concept called the *media mix*. The media mix is the relative weight given to the particular media. Certain media may be especially appropriate or inappropriate for a given product. For example, a product sold on looks and image (for example, makeup or beer) may do better in visual media such as television or magazines. On the other hand, if much technical information needs to be conveyed, then perhaps the print media may be better than broadcast. These sorts of issues, combined with cost and coverage, determine the media mix.

The media plan takes the media mix one step further, specifying exactly how the budget is to be spent within each of the media. This involves, among other things, the evaluation and selection of potential media schedules. These are the areas for which media models make their greatest contribution, and on which this book concentrates.

Evaluating Media Schedules

Before media schedules may be selected, there needs to be some way of evaluating the schedules. Criteria need to be employed that can objectively differentiate among different potential media vehicles or schedules. Thus it is important to measure the audiences of media vehicles, evaluate the reach and frequency of media schedules, and estimate the advertising response function.

Sissors and Surmanek summarize well the measurement of media audiences.[4] Scientific sampling methods are employed by research companies which measure audience size and composition. Their measurements are then used by advertisers as a guide to relative value of advertising time or space.

Techniques of measuring audiences are constantly evolving. For example, for years the standard source for network television data in the United States has been the A.C. Nielsen Company. It has used a combination of diaries and automatic recording devices to produce television ratings. Then AGB, a British company, introduced the "people meter" in the United States. This involves individual viewers pushing a button when they are watching a program. Advertisers received this new technology very favorably. In 1985, Nielsen announced that it too was converting to the new technology.

Given the audience measurements for individual media vehicles (and, when available, data on the joint audiences of pairs of vehicles), the media planner needs to extrapolate the audience's exposure to an entire media schedule. This is the task that media models do the best.

The reach and frequency of a media schedule must be evaluated (see chapter 2) with reach corresponding to the total number of people exposed, and frequency pertaining to the number of times exposed. The frequency distribution of exposure (see chapter 4) contains all of the information relevant to reach and frequency.

Given the frequency distribution of exposure, if the average response to a given number of ad exposures is known, then the total response to a schedule may be estimated. These response functions are difficult to obtain, and often the media planner must either resort to an assumed response function shape or conduct advertising experiments in test markets.

Selecting Media Vehicles

If a schedule may be evaluated, then, at least theoretically, the best schedule may be chosen. In practical problems, however, this often means considering such a large number of possible schedules that it is not feasible to evaluate them all. Thus, using the vehicle costs, a selection rule is employed, often using rapid calculation abilities of a computer (see chapter 5). In general, modern methods of evaluating and selecting media schedules rely heavily upon the computational power of modern computers.

One of the problems of determining media costs is that they are often the result of a bargaining process. Media vehicles are also often purchased in bundles, making it difficult to partial out the costs of particular vehicles. Nevertheless, for planning purposes, it is practical to provide cost estimates of vehicles and to use those to assist vehicle selection.

Selecting media schedules is as much art as science, and few would advocate turning the process entirely over to a computerized selection system. Still, it is at this point undeniable that computer evaluation and selection models may be used to advantage by savvy media planners, especially if they know the most important advantages and disadvantages of each method. This book is designed to assist the media planner in choosing relevant models to augment judgment in making media decisions.

References

1. Arnold M. Barban, Steven M. Cristol, and Frank J. Kopec, *Essentials of Media Planning* (Chicago: Crain Books, 1976).

2. Donald W. Jugenheimer and Peter B. Turk, *Advertising Media* (Columbus, Ohio: Grid, 1980).

3. Anthony F. McGann and J. Thomas Russell, *Advertising Media: A Managerial Approach* (Homewood, Ill.: Richard D. Irwin, 1981).

4. Jack Z. Sissors and Jim Surmanek, *Advertising Media Planning,* 2nd edition (Chicago: Crain Books, 1982).

5. Jim Surmanek, *Media Planning: A Quick and Easy Guide* (Chicago: Crain Books, 1980).

2
Estimating Total Audience: Reach Models

The first level of sophistication in the quantitative analysis of a media plan involves estimating a media schedule's reach and frequency. The term *reach* refers to the total number of people who are exposed to at least one of the ads in the schedule. Reach can be expressed either in total-number terms (ten million people) or more usefully in proportional terms (24 percent of the target population).

The term *frequency* refers to the average number of times an individual who was reached was exposed to the schedule. Thus *reach* refers to total penetration, while *frequency* refers to the depth of penetration.

Another related concept is *gross rating points* (GRPs), which refer to the total number of exposures generated by the schedule. This concept is related to reach and frequency by the equation

$$\text{GRPs} = \text{Reach} \cdot \text{Frequency} \tag{2.1}$$

Most media planners are now aware of reach and frequency, and the impact they have on the effectiveness of media schedules. It is surprising, however, to see how this knowledge is generally operationalized. Even college textbooks in media planning usually include tables from which to get reach from GRPs for particular media. These tables often produce numbers that are seriously in error! It is not possible mathematically to get reach from GRPs without having additional information or making strong assumptions.

This chapter presents legitimate methods for estimating reach, and exposes the assumptions underlying the methods. Many of these models are described in greater detail by Jean–Louis Chandon in his remarkable 1976 doctoral dissertation, *A Comparative Study of Media Exposure Models.*[5] His analyses of the older media models have been invaluable in preparing this manuscript.

Reach of One Vehicle

The following models apply to the situation of one media vehicle (such as a single television program, magazine, or radio show). For example, if an ad is shown on "Miami Vice" for four episodes, what percentage of the population will be exposed at least once to the ad?

The Binomial Model

This is the simplest model one could reasonably employ to estimate reach. Let p be the proportion of the population exposed, on average, to one insertion of the media vehicle. This value p then corresponds to rating for television or average issue audience for magazines, for example. Then if there are N insertions, the estimated reach, R_N, is simply

$$R_N = 1 - (1 - p)^N \tag{2.2}$$

Chandon empirically showed the inadequacy of the binomial model. It badly overestimated magazine reach. Research by this author confirms the bad results obtained by the binomial—an unsurprising finding considering the fact that the binomial treats all individuals in the population as though they were exactly the same.

The first great researcher in the media exposure area was Jean-Michel Agostini. In 1962, he devised the first good methods for estimating reach.[1,2] His formula is based on modeling $(R_N - R_{N-1})/(1 - R_{N-1})$ as approximately the power function a/Nb where a and b are empirically derived coefficients.

The resulting model is

$$R_N = R_{N-1} + (1 - R_{N-1}) \cdot (a/Nb) \tag{2.3}$$

where

$$a = R_1$$

and

$$b = [1/\ln(2)] \cdot \ln[R_1(1 - R_1)/(R_2 - R_1)]$$

In Chandon's dissertation, Agostini's model was as accurate empirically as any, with the exception of a few exotic models which would not be practical to implement due to unreasonable data or computational requirements. The Agostini model also has the bonus of providing reach estimates with no discernable bias.

Reach Tables

Much of this author's professional life has been spent devising better methods for obtaining reach, frequency, and related measures. More than once, reviewers have objected to this work on the basis that "these things are already readily available from tables." Such a statement is most likely to be made by a practitioner, and considering that the practitioners who review for journals are likely to be the best and most sophisticated, there appears to be a serious knowledge gap.

The tables they are referring to are the kind found in Sissors and Goodrich, *Media Planning Workbook.*[9] (See tables 2–1, 2–2, 2–3, and 2–4.)

Table 2–1
Reach of Four-Week Spot on Network Television (for TV Households Only)

4-Week HH GRP	*Spot Television*			*Network Television*	
	Daytime	*Prime*	*Fringe*	*Daytime*	*Prime*
100	34	50	43	43	61
200	53	70	65	55	81
300	63	80	77	58	85
400	69	87	83	60	90
600	70	92	88	70	92

Source: Jack Z. Sissors and William B. Goodrich, *Media Planning Workbook,* 2nd edition (Chicago: Crain Books, 1983), p. 67.

Table 2–2
Reach of Day Network Radio (Adults)

4-Week Adult GRP	*Percentage reach by number of networks*[a]						
	1	*2*	*3*	*4*	*5*	*6*	*7*
25	9	12	17	—	—	—	—
50	12	17	20	24	27	—	—
100	15	23	30	31	35	36	40
200	18	28	34	41	46	49	51
400	—	33	43	47	52	57	58
MAX	—	—	47	57	62	65	70

Source: Jack Z. Sissors and William B. Goodrich, *Media Planning Workbook,* 2nd edition (Chicago: Crain Books, 1983), p. 67.

[a]Very seldom would all radio networks be used.

Table 2–3
Reach of Spot Radio Drive Time

4-Week Adult GRP	Percentage Reach by Number of Stations 1	2	3	4	5	6	7+
50	19	—	—	—	—	—	—
100	21	32	—	—	—	—	—
200	26	38	47	55	62	—	—
400	30	47	54	63	67	71	73
MAX	—	—	60	70	75	80	85

Source: Jack Z. Sissors and William B. Goodrich, *Media Planning Workbook,* 2nd edition (Chicago: Crain Books, 1983), p. 67.

Table 2–4
Reach of Metro Daily Newspapers

Percentage Gross Circulation Coverage	Percentage Adult Reach by Number of Insertions in 4 Weeks 1	2	3	4	8	10	MAX
30	27	35	40	43	49	51	53
40	36	44	49	52	56	59	61
50	42	51	56	62	64	66	68
60	48	57	62	65	70	71	72
70	56	66	72	75	80	81	82
80	65	75	81	84	87	88	89

Source: Jack Z. Sissors and William B. Goodrich, *Media Planning Workbook,* 2nd edition (Chicago: Crain Books, 1983), p. 67.

These tables give estimated reach, given GRPs and perhaps one other variable. Obviously there is some serious averaging going on. Media planners less knowledgable than Sissors and Goodrich may not be aware of the inaccuracies inherent in such tables.

Averaging methods of the sort found in reach tables were first made respectable in 1965 by Engelman.[6] They produce seriously large errors because they treat every schedule with the same number of GRPs as though they were identical. Given the wide availability of computers, there is no longer any excuse for using such antiquated estimation techniques.

The Beta Binomial Model

In 1964, Richard Metheringham introduced a method that revolutionized media planning. His method is like the binomial in that each individual has a probability p of being exposed to an individual insertion. The novel element is that in the beta binomial model, the probability p is permitted to be different for each person. The distribution of p across the population is modeled as a beta distribution, a very flexible distribution which can closely approximate most unimodal distributions over the values of p between 0 and 1.

Reach may be estimated as

$$R_N = 1 - [(b + n - 1)(b + N - 2)\ldots (b)/(a + b + N - 1)\ldots(a + b)] \qquad (2.4)$$

where

$$a = \left(R_1R_2 - R_1^2\right) / \left(2R_1 - R_1^2 - R_2\right)$$

$$b = a(1 - R_1)/R_1$$

The Metheringham method became very popular, largely because of its ability to estimate the entire frequency distribution of exposure, which Agostini's method could not do. Nevertheless the beta binomial distribution (BBD) has some problems which should not be ignored.

For one thing its empirical performance is no better than the Agostini method's.[1] It also has the added disadvantages of an underestimation bias and the tendency to "blow up." "Blowing up" in this case means that the equations for a and b can give negative values, which leads to impossible results.

Reach of a Combination of Vehicles

When more than one vehicle is considered, the problem of estimating reach becomes somewhat more complex. As a result, specialized methods have been proposed to model this complexity.

The Sainsbury Formula

The Sainsbury formula is included in this book not because it is especially accurate (it is not), but because it seems to have obtained some popularity with practitioners.[4] It is essentially an extension of the binomial method to the case where the different vehicles are permitted to have different exposure probabilities.

If vehicles 1, 2, 3, . . . , etc. have exposure probabilities (ratings) $p_1, p_2, p_3, \ldots$, etc., then if these probabilities are independent and the population is homogeneous, reach may be calculated as simply the complement of non-exposure, or

$$R = 1 - [(1 - p_1)(1 - p_2)(1 - p_3) \ldots] \tag{2.5}$$

As is the case with the simple binomial model, the accuracy of this model is poor.

The Metheringham Model

As was stated in the previous section, Metheringham's model is really a beta binomial model. His method for obtaining the reach of a combination of vehicles is virtually identical to the previous one-vehicle reach formula. An additional simplifying assumption is required: that the vehicles be homogeneous. Thus the vehicles are treated as though they were different insertions of the same vehicle.

The model parameters are therefore averages across the vehicles in the schedule. With

$$R_1 = \left(\sum p_{ij}/N\right)$$

and

$$R_2 = (2R_1) - \left[\sum P_{ij}/(N(N - 1))\right]$$

with p_i representing the rating of vehicle i and p_{ij} the duplicated audience between vehicle i and vehicle j. This duplication is required to calculate Metheringham's reach estimate. If duplications are not available, then they must be estimated (see chapter 3).

The reach of the schedule is then calculated as in the previous section.

$$R = 1 - [(b + N - 1)(b + N - 2) \ldots (b)/(a + b + N - 1) \ldots (a + b)]$$

where

$$a = \left(R_1 R_2 - R_1^2 - R_1^2\right) / \left(2R_1 - R_1^2 - R_2\right)$$

and

$$b = a(1 - R_1)/R_1$$

Metheringham's formula has an overestimation bias,[5] but otherwise is reasonably accurate under normal circumstances. Of course its simplifying assumptions illuminate how and when the formula will fail. The assumption of homogeneous vehicles will be badly violated whenever a schedule is used in which there are both a high rated vehicle and a low rated vehicle, for example.

The Hofmans Formula

This formula is an extension of the Agostini formula.[7] Chandon reports it to be the most accurate reach formula among those he tested.[5] Nevertheless, like the Metheringham formula, it systematically overestimates reach.

Computationally we may obtain reach using Hofmans's formula as

$$R = \left(\sum p_i\right)^2 / \left[\left(\sum p_i\right) + \left(\sum k_{ij} p_{ij}\right)\right] \tag{2.6}$$

where

$$k_{ij} = (p_i + p_j)/(p_i + p_j - p_{ij}) \tag{2.7}$$

It has been suggested that if the duplications p_{ij} are not available, that the binomial estimates $p_i p_j$ be substituted.[3] Such a practice will result in the problems inherent in the binomial method, and should be used only as a last resort.

Conclusion

It should be clear that reliance upon reach tables (even if they are "legitimized" by being entered in computer memory) are ill advised, due to the availability of more sophisticated methods which are easy to implement.

If reach of one vehicle is to be obtained, the Agostini model appears to be the best choice, with the beta binomial model second. Each requires both vehicle audience and two-insertion reach. These data are generally available for national media, including television, but may not be available for small, local media vehicles. In that case published reach tables may be the last resort. When all else fails, the binomial model will yield very rough reach estimates.

If reach of a schedule containing two or more vehicles is to be obtained, then the Hofmans formula appears to be the best, again with Metheringham's beta binomial formula second. The Sainsbury formula and published reach tables should be avoided if possible.

References

1. Jean-Michel Agostini, "How to Estimate Unduplicated Audiences," *Journal of Advertising Research* (March 1961):11–14.

2. Jean-Michel Agostini, "Analysis of Magazine Accumulative Audience," *Journal of Advertising Research* (October 1962):24–27.

3. Marsha M. Boyd and John D. Leckenby, "Random Duplication in Reach/Frequency Estimation," *Current Issues and Research in Advertising,* ed. James H. Leigh and Claude R. Martin, Jr. (Ann Arbor: University of Michigan, 1985):95–114.

4. J.M. Caffyn and M. Sagovsky, "Net Audiences of British Newspapers: A Comparison of the Agostini and Sainsbury Methods," *Journal of Advertising Research* (March 1963):21–24.

5. Jean-Louis Chandon, *A Comparative Study of Media Exposure Models,* unpublished doctoral dissertation (Evanston, Ill.: Northwestern University, 1976).

6. F.L. Engelman, "An Empirical Formula for Audience Accumulation," *Journal of Advertising Research* (June 1965):21–28.

7. Pierre Hofmans, "Measuring the Cumulative Net Coverage of Any Combination of Media," *Journal of Marketing Research* (August 1966):269–78.

8. Richard A. Metheringham, "Measuring the Net Cumulative Coverage of a Print Campaign," *Journal of Advertising Research* (December 1964):23–28.

9. Jack Z. Sissors and William B. Goodrich, *Media Planning Workbook,* 2nd edition (Chicago: Crain Books, 1983), p. 67.

3
Estimating Audience Overlap: Duplication Models

Duplication refers to the overlap in the audiences of two or more vehicles. Overlap in the audiences of exactly two vehicles is *pairwise duplication*. Usually when people refer to duplication, they really mean pairwise duplication. Thus this chapter presents methods for estimating the duplicated audience of a pair of media vehicles.

Duplication is important because it affects the realization of media plans. For example if an advertising campaign is attempting to promote a new product, it will probably seek the largest possible audience, and hence, large reach. Duplication would preferably be low, given a set number of exposures (usually measured as GRPs).

On the other hand, the advertising campaign may wish to create a strong impression in a limited audience, perhaps to demonstrate a technical product, such as a camera. Such a campaign would desire low reach and high frequency, which would be achieved by having high duplication, given a particular number of exposures.

The reach models considered in chapter 2 embody assumptions concerning duplication; some authors (such as Chandon)[3] term those reach models *duplication models*. The distinction is made here because reach models necessarily use strong simplifying assumptions for their duplication estimates, while duplication models may be reasonably sophisticated and specialized. Duplication models do not necessarily make enough simplifying assumptions to permit expansion to an estimate for reach, although it is often the case that the estimated duplications may be used as inputs to other models which estimate reach and/or the frequency distribution of exposure.

Types of Media Vehicle Pairs

This chapter will emphasize specialized methods for estimating the duplication of media vehicles for which extensive data are readily available. The general concepts underlying these models may easily be adapted to other

Table 3–1
Duplication Estimation Methods Classified by Media and Segmentation

Media (Pair Type)	*Total Population*	*Target Market*
TV (cross-pair)	Goodhardt–Ehrenberg (1969) Headen–Klompmaker–Rust (1979)	(present study)
TV (self-pair)	Headen–Klompmaker–Rust (1979) Rice–Leckenby (1984) (present study)	(present study)
Magazine (cross-pair)	(readily available)	Cannon (1983) (present study)
Magazine (self-pair)	(readily available)	(present study)
TV–Magazine	Rust–Leone (1984)	(present study)

Source: Roland T. Rust, Robert P. Leone, and Mary R. Zimmer, "Estimating the Duplicated Audience of Media Vehicles in National Advertising Schedules," working paper. Austin, Texas: University of Texas.

related media. The media examined here are network television and national consumer magazines, which are the most important media for many national advertisers.

Table 3–1 (adapted from Rust, Leone, and Zimmer)[13] illustrates a typology for duplication in these media. Duplication may be estimated for the entire population or for a particular target market. Considerable empirical work has been done on total population duplication, but to most advertisers the duplication of audience in a particular target market is more important. This chapter examines models for both cases.

Television program pairs may be either *cross-pairs* or *self-pairs*. Cross-pairs are program pairs involving two different programs (for example, "Dallas" and "60 Minutes"), while self-pairs involve two episodes of the same program (such as "Dallas" both this week and next week). The same distinction is made for magazine pairs.

Television–magazine pairs involve one television program and one magazine.

Total Population Duplication

There were two notable pioneering approaches to the modeling of duplication. The first, by Goodhardt[5] and Goodhardt and Ehrenberg[6] involved a simple empirical observation: that the duplicated audience was approximately proportional to the product of the ratings of the vehicles. In symbols, this is

$$p_{ij} = Kp_ip_j \tag{3.1}$$

where p_{ij} is the duplicated audience, K is a constant, and p_i and p_j are the ratings of the vehicles (in proportional terms). The authors assumed an almost religious devotion to this simple model, going so far as to call the mathematical relationship a law, akin to the laws of physics.[4] Nevertheless the empirical validation of this relationship was sorely lacking, as will be seen later in the chapter. Still, their model was a useful first step in modeling duplication.

At about the same time, renowned operations researcher John Little, with his student Leonard Lodish, developed a model (discussed more extensively in chapter 5) for selecting media vehicles.[9] Hacking through the convoluted mathematics for which those authors are known yields a relatively simple duplication formula of the form

$$p_{ij} = (p_ip_j)^K \tag{3.2}$$

This model also has problems empirically, as will be seen. It is similar to the Goodhardt–Ehrenberg model in that it assumes that a constant will do a good job of estimating duplication.

Television Cross-Pair Duplication

The Goodhardt–Ehrenberg model was first used to estimate the duplicated audiences of television program pairs.[6] It makes one allowance for the complexity of the media environment: employing one K for program pairs on the same channel, and a different K for program pairs on different channels. Goodhardt and Ehrenberg defend the accuracy of their model on the basis that the duplicated audience (in rating points) is small. This is not a convincing argument, however, because the duplications are usually quite small themselves. Thus a small error in absolute terms may be unacceptably large in proportional terms.

Early empirical testing was performed on British television,[7] but further work was subsequently done on American television by Barwise and Ehrenberg.[1]

The Goodhardt–Ehrenberg model has been tested more critically by other authors. Chandon used a statistical test to empirically demonstrate that the "constant" K was not really constant, within sampling error.[3]

Robert Headen, Jay Klompmaker, and this author developed an extension of the Goodhardt–Ehrenberg model, one designed to model some of the variables present in the television environment.[8] Our model had a different mathematical form, but it was conceptually similar to the Goodhardt–Ehrenberg approach. The additional variables were whether or not the programs had the same program type (for example, sports or news), whether the programs had the same daypart (time of day broadcast), and whether the two vehicles were two episodes of the same program. In mathematical notation, the model is expressed as

$$p_{ij} = b_0(b_1^{X_1})(b_2^{X_2})(b_3^{X_3}) \cdot (b_4^{X_4})(p_i p_j) \cdot e^u \qquad (3.3)$$

where the bs are regression coefficients, X_1 is a dummy variable indicating whether the two vehicles are on the same channel, and X_2, X_3, and X_4 are dummy variables indicating whether the two episodes have the same program type, daypart, and program, respectively.

The expanded model, incorporating the new variables, performed significantly better, both statistically and substantively.[11] The model is general enough to accommodate both cross-pairs and self-pairs. However the data used to estimate and validate the model were primarily comprised of cross-pairs, and thus its performance on self-pairs was not really addressed by that study. Nevertheless it is clear that for television cross-pairs, the Headen–Klompmaker–Rust model performs the best.

Television Self-Pair Duplication

Descriptive accounts of television self-pair duplication patterns, along with limited empirical results, have been presented by Goodhardt, Ehrenberg, and Collins[7] and by Barwise and Ehrenberg.[1] These authors do not present an explicit model which could be used generally to estimate self-pair duplication. The Headen–Klompmaker–Rust model cited in the previous section provides self-pair duplication estimates, but until recently had not been tested on self-pair data.

The first published model with the explicit intent to estimate self-pair duplication for television was devised by Rice and Leckenby.[10] Their model is based on the general form of the Goodhardt–Ehrenberg duplication constant. They estimate duplication as

$$p_{ii} = k_i(p_i)^2 \qquad (3.4)$$

where p_{ii} represents self-pair duplication, and the multiplier k_i is adjusted according to program rating and "program type."

Their program type variable actually includes both program type and daypart components. Thus a complete specification of their prediction model might be written as

$$\ln(k_i/(A - k_i) = b_0 + b_1 p_i + \sum c_i X_i + \sum d_j Y_j \qquad (3.5)$$

where the X_is are program type dummy variables (with coefficients c_i), the Y_js are daypart dummy variables (with coefficients d_j), and A is an empirically derived upper asymptote. Data limitations did not permit the use of such a complete model in their empirical work. However telephone conversations and correspondence confirm that this extension of their model is consistent with their thinking.

Robert Leone, Mary Zimmer, and this author have proposed another model for television self-pair duplication, again along the general conceptual lines of the Goodhardt–Ehrenberg approach. Using the above notation, the model is

$$p_{ii} = b_0\left(p_1{}^2\right)^{b_1} \cdot \prod_i \left(c_i{}^{X_i}\right) \cdot \prod_j \left(d_j{}^{Y_j}\right) \qquad (3.6)$$

where the X_is are program type dummy variables (such as $X_6 = 1$ if the program is a news program), the Y_js are daypart dummy variables (for example, $Y_4 = 1$ if the program is aired in prime time), and the c_is and d_js are coefficients.

This model was tested against the Headen–Klompmaker–Rust and Rice–Leckenby models.[13] The Rust–Leone–Zimmer model was found to slightly outperform the Headen–Klompmaker–Rust model and to do much better than the Rice–Leckenby model.

It was found that (even allowing for the extra estimated parameters) it was better to estimate two separate forms of the Rust–Leone–Zimmer model. Different coefficients were estimated for two cases: same week and different weeks.

The best model specification for estimating the duplicated audience of the same-week self-pair sample includes the program rating and program type variables, but deletes daypart. The different-week model includes the program rating and daypart variables, but deletes program type.

The empirical evidence suggests that the Rust–Leone–Zimmer model is the preferable model for estimating television self-pair duplication.

Magazine Duplication

Duplication data for national consumer magazines are readily available from sources such as SMRB (formerly Simmons) and MRI (Mediamark). Therefore no total population duplication models are required.

Television–Magazine Duplication

Little work has been done regarding television–magazine duplication. The only published estimation method was devised by Robert Leone and this author.[12] The Goodhardt–Ehrenberg framework has again been applied, estimating

$$p_{ij} = k_{ij}p_ip_j$$

where p_i is the television show's audience size, p_j is the average audience for the magazine, and k_{ij} is a multiplier depending upon the historically observed duplication between magazine j and the program type of television program i. The rationale behind this method is that magazines tend to be relatively long-lived, as do program types. Thus although individual programs may come and go, their audience overlap with any particular magazine may be approximated by the historical duplications observed for that program's program type.

This model is recommended only because it is the only one available. While it seems sound conceptually, adequate empirical testing has not been done because this model was not the focus of the paper in which it appeared.

Target Market Duplication

Target market duplication refers to the duplication of audience observed within a particular target market (such as women ages eighteen to forty-nine). Because advertisers commonly express their marketing objectives in terms of target markets, it is useful to estimate media exposure within the target market. Duplication data are rarely available for target markets, even in magazines, which makes duplication estimation models essential.

The Cannon Model

Hugh Cannon did the pioneering research in target market duplication.[2] Denoting the target market audiences as m_i and m_j, and target market duplication as m_{ij}, Cannon estimates the target market duplication as

$$m_{ij} = [p_{ij}(m_i + m_j)/(p_i + p_j)] \tag{3.7}$$

where again p_{ij} is the total population duplication, and p_i and p_j are the audience sizes of the two vehicles.

This is an ad hoc approach, but it yields reasonable empirical results. The conceptual basis may be more easily visualized by rewriting equation 3.7 as

$$m_{ij}/(m_i + m_j) = p_{ij}/(p_i + p_j).$$

Thus there is an independence of sorts being hypothesized, in the sense that the ratio of duplicated audience to the sum of the audience is assumed to be the same for a target market as it is for the total population. Cannon devised his method for magazine duplication, but there is no reason that it cannot be used for other media.

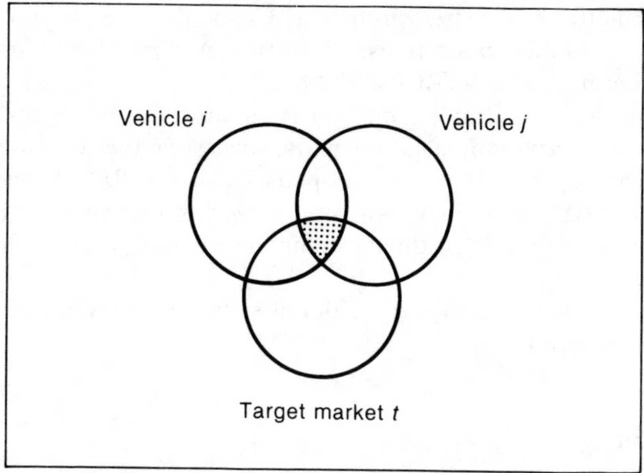

Source: Roland T. Rust, Robert P. Leone, and Mary R. Zimmer, "Estimating the Duplicated Audience of Media Vehicles in National Advertising Schedules," working paper. Austin, Texas: University of Texas.

Figure 3–1. A Pictorial Representation of Target Market Duplication

The Rust–Leone–Zimmer Model

A new approach to estimating target market duplication emerges if the target market duplication is conceptualized in a different way. Figure 3–1, adapted from Rust, Leone and Zimmer,[13] suggests the possible usefulness of treating the target market t as though it were a third media vehicle. The target market duplication problem then becomes one of finding the common overlap of the three vehicles, and the estimation assumes a symmetric nature.

An ugly (but not difficult) derivation yields, in the notation used above for Cannon's model

$$m_{ij} = \tfrac{1}{3}\{[(r_j r_t r_{ij} m_{it}) + (r_i r_t r_{ij} m_{jt}) + (r_i r_j r_t m_{it} m_{jt})]/(r_i r_j r_t)\}. \quad (3.8)$$

Empirical Results

Cannon[2] did a limited empirical study, apparently just for the purpose of illustrating that the estimates obtained were not unreasonable. His assertion that the estimates are unbiased is unjustified, and result from an error in the calculation of his t statistic.

Recently a more complete empirical study has been done[13] on a variety of media combinations. In the magazine cross-pair case, the situation for which Cannon's method was originally devised, the Rust–Leone–Zimmer method performs significantly better. Ironically Cannon's method appears much better suited for other applications. His method performs better for television self-pairs and magazine self-pairs.

The Rust–Leone–Zimmer method is significantly better for magazine cross-pairs and television–magazine pairs, suggesting that Cannon's method may be generally preferable for self-pairs, with the Rust–Leone–Zimmer method working better for cross-pairs. The case of television cross-pairs yields inconclusive results, although Cannon's method is better on one error criterion.

Both of the methods show a small but significant bias in their estimates across all pair types.

Conclusion

Table 3–2, adapted from Rust, Leone, and Zimmer,[13] gives a "user's guide" for selecting a duplication estimation model, based on the results of empirical research. It is interesting to observe that all of the recommended models have been devised no earlier than 1979. Detailed sources for each of these models are listed in the references below.

Table 3–2
Suggested Duplication Estimation Models by Usage Situation

Media (Pair Type)	*Total Population*	*Target Market*
TV (cross-pair)	Headen–Klompmaker–Rust (1979)	Cannon (1983)[b]
TV (self-pair)	(proposed TV self-pair model)[a]	Cannon (1983)[b]
Magazine (cross-pair)	(readily available)	(proposed target market model)[a]
Magazine (self-pair)	(readily available)	Cannon (1983)[b]
TV–Magazine	Rust–Leone (1984)	(proposed target market model)[a]

Source: Roland T. Rust, Robert P. Leone, and Mary R. Zimmer, "Estimating the Duplicated Audience of Media Vehicles in National Advertising Schedules," working paper. Austin, Texas: University of Texas.

[a]New model.

[b]New application of old model.

References

1. T.P. Barwise and A.S.C. Ehrenberg, *Television and Its Audience: Recent Research at the LBS* (London: London Business School, May 1984).

2. Hugh M. Cannon, "Reach and Frequency Estimates for Specialized Target Markets," *Journal of Advertising Research* (June–July 1983):45–50.

3. Jean–Louis Chandon, *A Comparative Study of Media Exposure Models,* unpublished doctoral dissertation (Evanston, Ill.: Northwestern University, 1976).

4. A.S.C. Ehrenberg, "Laws in Marketing—A Tailpiece," *Applied Statistics* (1966), 257–67.

5. G.J. Goodhardt, "The Constant in Duplicated Television Viewing," *Nature* (December 1966):1616.

6. G.J. Goodhardt and A.S.C. Ehrenberg, "Duplication of Viewing between and within Channels," *Journal of Marketing Research* (May 1969), 169–78.

7. G.J. Goodhardt, A.S.C. Ehrenberg, and M.A. Collins, *The Television Audience: Patterns of Viewing* (Lexington, Mass.: Lexington Books, 1975).

8. Robert S. Headen, Jay E. Klompmaker, and Roland T. Rust, "The Duplication of Viewing Law and Television Media Schedule Evaluation," *Journal of Marketing Research* (August 1979):333–40.

9. John D.C. Little and Leonard M. Lodish, "A Media Planning Calculus," *Operations Research* (January–February 1969):1–35.

10. Marshall D. Rice and John D. Leckenby, "Predicting Within-Vehicle Television Duplication," *Proceedings of the American Academy of Advertising* (1984).

11. Roland T. Rust, Jay E. Klompmaker, and Robert S. Headen, "A Comparative Study of Television Duplication Models," *Journal of Advertising* (1981):42–46.

12. Roland T. Rust and Robert P. Leone, "The Mixed Media Dirichlet Multinomial Distribution: A Model for Evaluating Television–Magazine Advertising Schedules," *Journal of Marketing Research* (February 1984):84–99.

13. Roland T. Rust, Robert P. Leone, and Mary R. Zimmer, "Estimating the Duplicated Audience of Media Vehicles in National Advertising Schedules," working paper, University of Texas at Austin.

4
Estimating Frequency of Exposure

Old school media planners are satisfied to describe frequency of exposure in terms of reach and average frequency. Actually though, there is much more to frequency of exposure than this.

As an example, suppose that out of a population of ten people, three are exposed to the media schedule. One of the three is exposed ten times, and the other two are exposed only once. The reach in this case would be 3 (or .3 in proportionate terms), while the average frequency would be $12 \div 3 = 4$. One would expect that the person with ten exposures has been very effectively exposed, while the other two people may not have been affected much.

Krugman hypothesized that three exposures were necessary to effectively expose an individual to an advertisement.[10] This concept of *effective exposure* has in recent years gained some acceptance among practitioners. Using Krugman's guideline, in the above example one of the ten people would be effectively exposed.

Now imagine another ten people, of whom three were each exposed four times. The reach and average frequency would be identical to the previous case. Yet this time three would be effectively exposed! This illustrates that reach and average frequency do not give us enough information about exposure. It is advisable to obtain information about the *distribution* of the frequency of exposure.

Fortunately there has been considerable work on estimating frequency distributions of exposure. Modern media services and advertising agencies estimate frequency distributions to evaluate proposed media schedules.

A study by Leckenby and Kishi documents the extent to which advanced methods of estimating frequency distributions are used.[11] Their study showed that 77 percent of media planners requested frequency distribution results. Interestingly, 45 percent of the client personnel also requested frequency distribution information. They also found that 49 percent of advertising agencies sampled used two or more methods of estimating the frequency distribution. Their findings are echoed by Guggenheim, who states, "There's hardly an advertising media department today that does not have access to a wide variety of media planning and evaluative computer models."[6]

The concept of effective exposure is currently popular as a means of assessing a frequency distribution. Even better is the concept of a response function. In effect (given that, say, three exposures are considered effective) zero exposures, one exposure, and two exposures are all considered worthless. Then, all of a sudden, at three exposures the advertisement becomes effective, and then can become no more effective regardless of how many subsequent exposures there are. The response function approach, on the other hand, permits relative degrees of effectiveness. For example the effectiveness could increase with every exposure, up to a point of saturation. Thus four exposures might be better than three exposures by some slight amount.

The evaluation of frequency distributions using response functions will be considered in greater detail in chapter 5. For our present purposes, let it suffice to say that frequency distributions yield information to the media planner that can be used to evaluate schedules, using either effective exposure or response functions.

There are two main types of frequency of exposure models, corresponding to the availability of data. The first type of model requires pairwise duplications between the vehicles. These may be measured (as in national magazines) or estimated (as in the case of television). The second type of model (usually used for television) does not require duplication data.

Models Requiring Duplications

Beta Binomial Models

Chapter 2 discussed Metheringham's method for estimating reach. His method, involving the beta binomial distribution, may also be used to estimate the entire frequency distribution of exposure.[15]

If

$$A = \sum R_i \tag{4.1}$$

$$D = \sum_{i \neq j} R_{ij} \tag{4.2}$$

where the R_is are the (proportional) audiences and the R_{ij}s are the duplications, then given n vehicles in the schedule, the beta binomial parameters a and b are estimated as

$$a = [2DA - A^2(n - 1)]/[A^2(n - 1) - 2Dn] \tag{4.3}$$

$$b = a(n - A)/A \tag{4.4}$$

The frequency distribution of exposure is then estimated as

$$f(x) = [\Gamma(n + 1) \cdot \Gamma(a + b) \cdot \Gamma(a + x) \cdot \Gamma(n + b - x)] /$$

$$[\Gamma(x + 1) \cdot \Gamma(n - x + 1) \cdot \Gamma(a) \cdot G(b) \cdot \Gamma(a + b + n)] \quad (4.5)$$

where x is the number of exposures, $f(x)$ is the frequency of x exposures, and Γ is the gamma function. This expression conveniently expresses the frequencies solely in terms of gamma functions. Computational subroutines for calculating gamma functions are available in numerical analysis packages such as IMSL.

Metheringham's method is still popular, but users should be aware of its assumptions and limitations. Each individual in the population is assumed to have a fixed probability of being exposed to any particular vehicle in the schedule. Notice that this means that vehicles are for all practical purposes considered to be identical! The advantage of Metheringham's beta binomial is that individuals across the population may have different probabilities p. A continuous probability distribution of these ps is assumed to exist, modeled by a beta distribution.

While the Metheringham method usually works reasonably well, there are some empirical quirks which must be considered. First, there is the phenomenon of declining reach. (Note that in terms of a frequency distribution, reach $= 1 - f(0)$.) Declining reach means that it is possible to construct an example for which adding an additional vehicle to the schedule would produce a lower reach estimate! Second, there is the systematic tendency for the model to overestimate reach, or, in other words, underestimate $f(0)$. Third, the model does not do well if there is a bimodal distribution of the probabilities p, such as might occur if there were two distinct viewer segments.

Schreiber demonstrated that individual media habits may be unstable (*nonstationary* in statistics jargon), which implies that the individual's p probability may change over time.[20] Sabavala and Morrison built a beta binomial model which permitted the p value to change.[19] Their simplifying assumption, that what the p value was before is not related to what it is now, seems unreasonable, and limits the practical value of their model.

The Beta Matrix Method

The beta matrix method is a rather odd ad hoc procedure which has gained some popularity. It was proposed by Greene and Stock,[5] and has been used by Simmons.[21] A good description is given by Chandon.[3]

The beta matrix method analyzes two vehicles at a time. Audience exposure levels and duplications are displayed in a matrix (table). The idea is that if we assume that the rows and columns of the table are each generated according to a beta binomial distribution (an utterly atheoretical assumption), then the beta binomial a and b parameters may be obtained (using $n = 2$). Then if there are, for example, five insertions in the first vehicle instead of two, the columns are estimated using the a and b parameters derived above, only with $n = 5$.

If the second vehicle has more than two insertions, four for example, then the expanded matrix is reanalyzed to obtain the new row a and b parameters, and then extended like the columns, using the a and b parameters and $n = 4$.

Finding the beta binomial parameters for a row or column is fairly straightforward. Starting with the row (or column) mean and variance,

$$\mu = \sum x f(x) \tag{4.6}$$

$$\sigma^2 = \sum (x - \mu)^2 f(x) \tag{4.7}$$

the beta binomial parameters a and b may be obtained[8]

$$a = \mu[\sigma^2 - (n - \mu)]/[\mu(n - \mu) - n\sigma^2] \tag{4.8}$$

$$b = a(n - \mu)/\mu \tag{4.9}$$

Expansion to an increased n is then accomplished using the formulas of the previous section.

The beta matrix method has limitations also. Of greatest concern is that depending on whether the row or column is expanded first (for the case of more than two exposures in each vehicle), there can be different estimates. Given a large problem (multiple insertions in several vehicles), the problem quickly gets out of hand in terms of the amount of computation required. Thus for theoretical and practical reasons the beta matrix method is not recommended.

Occasionally it is argued that the beta matrix, even considering its ad hoc nature and cumbersome calculations, is preferable to the beta binomial because the beta matrix can accommodate multiple insertions in each vehicle. This underestimates the beta binomial.

It is possible to model multiple insertions with the beta binomial by considering each insertion to be a different vehicle. Then the self-pair duplication is simply considered across-pair, and computation proceeds normally.

Dirichlet Models

The Dirichlet distribution is the multivariate extension of the beta distribution. It also yields the Dirichlet multinomial distribution (DMD) as the multivariate extension of the beta binomial distribution (BBD).

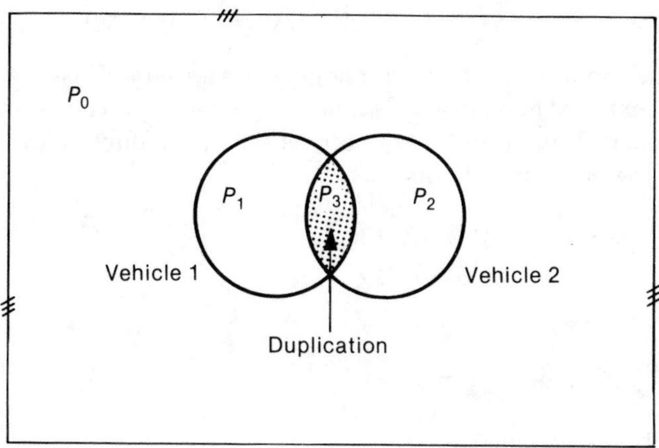

Figure 4–1. Exposure Possibilities for Two Media Vehicles

In the BBD models (for example, Metheringham) individuals are permitted to have different probabilities of exposure. However the vehicles in the media schedule are assumed to be identical. The idea behind using the Dirichlet distribution is to allow exposure to different vehicles to be different.

Chandon first suggested the use of the Dirichlet for this purpose.[3] Figure 4–1, adapted from Chandon, illustrates one individual's exposure possibilities for two vehicles. (This is easily extended to three or more vehicles.) If there is one insertion in each vehicle, then this figure shows all of the exposure possibilities. Now suppose that there are two insertions in each vehicle. Chandon proposes to sample twice from that diagram (sample space). Actually the technique does not really work theoretically, because the two "trials" are not really independent. This theoretical problem casts serious doubt on all Dirichlet media models, although the good empirical results generally obtained may cause us to have less concern.

The Chandon model is limited to situations involving two vehicles. Another problem with Chandon's idea is that there must be the same number of insertions in each vehicle, seriously restricting the model's applicability. (This is also a problem with Leckenby's model, but not the Rust–Leone mixed-media model discussed later in the chapter.)

So far the diagram and discussion relate to just one individual. The probabilities of the regions in the diagram (of which there are four in the two-vehicle case) are that individual's probabilities of exposure. The Dirichlet distribution permits a multivariate distribution of these probabilities across the population.

First the beta binomial parameters are obtained, as with the beta matrix method. Then the weighted average of their sum is obtained:

$$S = [R_1(a_1 + b_1) + R_2(a_2 + b_2)]/(R_1 + R_2) \qquad (4.10)$$

where the *a*s and *b*s are the beta binomial parameters. Then, denoting the proportion exposed to neither as P_0, the proportion exposed to only vehicle 1 or only vehicle 2 as P_1 and P_2 respectively, and the duplication as P_3, the Dirichlet parameters are obtained as

$$A_0 = P_0 \cdot S$$
$$A_1 = P_1 \cdot S$$
$$A_2 = P_2 \cdot S$$
$$A_3 = P_3 \cdot S$$

where the *P*s are obtained as

$$P_0 = 1 - R_1 - R_2 + R_{12}$$
$$P_1 = R_1 - R_{12}$$
$$P_2 = R_2 - R_{12}$$
$$P_3 = R_{12}$$

Given the Dirichlet parameters, the joint exposure probabilities $f(x_1,x_2)$ (where x_1 is number of exposures to vehicle 1 and x_2 is number of exposures to vehicle 2) are estimated as

$$f(x_1,x_2) = n! \cdot \Gamma\left(\sum A_i\right) \cdot \prod[\Gamma(x_i + A_i)] / \prod(x_i!) \cdot \prod[\Gamma(A_i)] \cdot \Gamma\left(n + \sum A_i\right) \qquad (4.11)$$

The Leckenby–Kishi model[11] builds upon ideas first explored by Chandon.[3] Following Chandon, they first estimate a univariate exposure distribution on the exposure diagram resulting from one insertion in each vehicle (corresponding in the two-vehicle case to figure 4–1, with the exception that the P_1 and P_2 regions would be combined). Thus the events considered are zero exposures, one exposure, two exposures, etc.

They then repeatedly sample from these events, producing a univariate frequency distribution. The joint frequency distribution is not estimated. Also the method is restricted to situations in which there are equal numbers of insertions in each vehicle. The last assumption can be relaxed, but only by assuming that each insertion is a different vehicle, which in effect uses only the preliminary univariate estimation and does away with any use of the Dirichlet.

Computationally any non-Dirichlet exposure model (for example, the beta binomial) may be used to estimate the exposure probabilities for one insertion in each vehicle. Leckenby and Kishi use a method proposed by Hofmans.[9] The first step yields probabilities P_0, P_1, P_2, etc., which are the probabilities of no exposures, one exposure, two exposures, etc., to a schedule containing one insertion in each vehicle.

Obtaining the Dirichlet parameters is then the same procedure derived by Chandon. The Leckenby–Kishi parameters do not have the same meaning, however. Only the univariate frequency distribution may be produced, by use of some fairly involved enumeration of possibilities which will not be reproduced here. The general idea is to find the event combinations that produce a particular number of exposures and then sum up those event combinations' probabilities.

Simulation Models

In the 1960s, researchers were becoming aware that finding good models to estimate frequency distributions of exposure was tougher than they thought. They were also in the initial euphoria of the computer revolution, and methods substituting brute force computing for mathematical cleverness were in vogue.

Simulation models represented the epitome of reliance upon brute force computing power. The most notable simulation model was the one proposed by Gensch.[4] Other simulation models followed, some resembling the Gensch model quite closely. At least one major advertising agency still uses one.

Gensch's model, AD–ME–SIM, uses a large number of personal media probabilities, obtained from tabulation of a computer tape containing a large syndicated data base, preferably based on a national sample. Each individual would be assigned a probability, based on previous exposure, of being exposed to a particular vehicle.

This method certainly relaxes almost all of the restrictive assumptions which plague the more mathematical models. Unfortunately advertising agencies desiring to test a handful of potential schedules may have to run their computer all night. If they have more than a handful of schedules to evaluate or if they have to pay for their computer time, this method can become prohibitively expensive and time consuming.

The AD–ME–SIM model was also developed to be a media selection model. Those aspects will be discussed further in chapter 5.

Models not Requiring Duplications

Generally speaking, modeling television exposure demands the use of models that do not require duplications as an input, because such duplications are not generally available. The only way around this is to first estimate the duplications and then use the estimates in a model that requires duplications.

The Binomial Model

The simplest thing to do is to assume that all of the vehicles in the schedule are independent of one another, but are identical. These are obviously very bad assumptions. The frequency of exposure estimates are then

$$f(x) = C(n,x) \cdot p^x(1 - p)^{n-x} \tag{4.12}$$

where $C(n,x)$ is the combinational "n choose x," n is the number of vehicles, x is the number of exposures, and p is the average rating (in proportional terms) of the n vehicles. Again, there is no problem if there are multiple insertions within vehicles. Each insertion is considered its own vehicle.

This method yields extremely poor results, and should be avoided whenever possible. For example Chandon shows that on magazine data the binomial model overestimates reach $(1 - f(0))$ by an average of 31 percent![3]

The Revised Binomial Model

Using the binomial distribution is appealing because it is so simple. With this in mind, Balachandra[2] and Aaker[1] developed a new way to employ the binomial. The basic idea is that n and p are both fit to the data. Thus n is not necessarily the number of vehicles and p is not necessarily the average rating, which makes this model rather odd from a theoretical perspective.

First the mean and variance of the ratings are calculated:

$$\mu = \sum r_i$$
$$\sigma^2 = \sum r_i(1 - r_i)$$

Then, the n and p are found which fit these moments, and thus solve the following system of equations:

$$\mu = np = \sum r_i$$
$$\sigma^2 = np(1 - p) = \sum r_i(1 - r_i)$$

yielding the solution

$$n = \mu^2/(\mu - \sigma^2)$$
$$p = \mu/n$$

This looks innocent enough, but there are still a couple of annoyances to be dealt with. First, there is no assurance that n will be a whole number, which it has to be to employ the binomial formula. In practice this means rounding to the nearest whole number.

Second, whenever σ^2 is greater than μ, as can happen with even fairly normal-looking schedules, the parameters are negative and the frequency distribution blows up.

Also, the revised binomial method does very poorly empirically, compared to the other models discussed in this section (with the obvious exception of the simple binomial model).

The Headen–Klompmaker–Teel Beta Binomial Model

The University of North Carolina was a hotbed of media models research in the late 1970s. Robert Headen and Jay Klompmaker teamed with doctoral student Jesse Teel on several models. When Teel graduated, this author was delighted to assume his spot.

Headen, Klompmaker, and Teel devised a method of estimating a beta binomial distribution without requiring duplications.[8] They tested it in several television applications, including spot and network.

Given a schedule of n vehicles, they postulate a probability p^*, which represents the average probability of exposure for an individual to any spot in the schedule. This sounds similar to the binomial model, especially in that the vehicles are considered homogeneous. However, as in the Metheringham method, the individual probabilities p^* are allowed to vary across the population. In fact, the basic Metheringham equations apply here too, with the exception that the estimation is different.

The H–K–T method arrives at the beta binomial parameters a and b by the method of moments. The mean of the beta binomial is simply the sum of the (proportional) ratings

$$\mu = \sum r_i = na/(a + b)$$

and the variance of the beta binomial is estimated using a predictive equation which exploits characteristics of the schedule. The general form used is

$$\sigma^2 = A(X_1{}^{B_1})(X_2{}^{B_2})(X_3{}^{B_3})(X_4{}^{B_4})e$$

$$= nab(n + a + b)/[(a + b)^2(a + b + 1)] \qquad (4.13)$$

where

X_1 = number of vehicles in the schedule
X_2 = number of TV stations used
X_3 = number of TV stations available
X_4 = average rating in the schedule
e = the regression error term

The variance regression is estimated using either a linear regression obtained by taking logarithms of both sides, or (more correctly) by a nonlinear regression. The two equations are then solved simultaneously for a and b, with the solution being

$$a = \mu\{[n\sigma^2/\mu(n - \mu)] - n\}/n\{1 - [n\sigma^2/\mu(n - \mu)]\}$$

$$b = a(n - \mu)/\mu$$

Operationalization of the model is sometimes misunderstood. The variance regression does not need to be performed for every schedule. It may be calibrated periodically on representative schedules, using syndicated data, such as SMRB. The coefficients obtained may then be used on a routine basis to get the beta binomial parameters for schedules.

The Headen–Klompmaker–Teel beta binomial model yielded reasonably good empirical results, but it is bettered by the newer models discussed subsequently.

The Rust–Klompmaker Model

The beta binomial parameters a and b are actually the parameters of the beta distribution which is compounded with the binomial to produce the beta binomial. Thus it would be more elegant conceptually to estimate the beta parameters from the moments of the beta rather than the beta binomial. This is the approach used in the Rust–Klompmaker model. Otherwise this model is conceptually similar to the Headen–Klompmaker–Teel model.

For technical reasons discussed elsewhere[16] the parameters estimated are μ, the mean of the beta, and V^*, which is defined as

$$V^* = \mu(1 - \mu) - \sigma^2 \tag{4.14}$$

where σ^2 is the variance of the beta. It should be pointed out that the mean and variance of the beta are not in general equal to the mean and variance of the beta binomial, which means the symbols used in this subsection are not equivalent to the symbols in the previous subsection.

The parameter μ is simply the average rating in the schedule

$$\mu = \left(\sum r_i\right)/n$$

and V^* is obtained using a regression equation. Again, only one regression need be performed, and then its coefficient estimates used repeatedly for subsequent schedules.

The regression equation for estimating V^* is

$$V^* = A(1 + X_1)^{B_1}(1 + X_2)^{B_2}(1 + X_3)^{B_3}(1 + X_4)^{B_4} \cdot X_5{}^{B_5}X_6{}^{B_6}X_7{}^{B_7}e \qquad (4.15)$$

where

$A, B_1, \ldots B_7$ are coefficients
e is the regression error term
X_1 = proportion of same-channel pairs
X_2 = proportion of same-daypart pairs
X_3 = proportion of same-program-type pairs
X_4 = proportion of self-pairs
X_5 = average rating
X_6 = variance of the ratings
X_7 = number of vehicles in the schedule

As additional explanation, the proportion of same-channel pairs, for example, is the proportion of all possible pairs of programs in the schedule that are programs on the same channel.

The Rust–Klompmaker model generally performs better empirically than the Headen–Klompmaker–Teel model.[16] The differences are statistically and practically significant, but are fairly small.

The Leckenby–Rice Beta Binomial Model

Another beta binomial approach is proposed by Leckenby and Rice.[13] This approach is a two-stage procedure which first estimates the reach, using a high estimate and a low estimate, and then estimates the beta binomial using the method of means and zeros.

The high estimate for reach is obtained as

$$RU = 1 - \prod(1 - p_i)^{n_i} \qquad (4.16)$$

where the product is over the vehicles i in the schedule, given their proportional ratings p_i. The low estimate is given as

$$RL = 1 - \prod(1 - p_i) \qquad (4.17)$$

The RU and RL are then averaged to get the reach estimate. There is no good theoretical reason for doing this, and in fact there may be good reasons for not doing this. One questionable feature, for example, is that the low reach estimate does not change, regardless of the number of insertions in each vehicle. Each vehicle could have one insertion or a million, and the same low estimate would be obtained. This is clearly undesirable.

They tested their method against the Headen–Klompmaker–Teel method using two hundred schedules tabulated from SMRB, with favorable empirical results. Inexplicably they did not test their method against the Rust–Klompmaker method, which in a previously published study[16] had also performed better than Headen–Klompmaker–Teel.

The Estimated Duplication Approach

An alternative way to handle the absence of duplication data is to estimate the duplications. There is no published attempt to do this, but preliminary findings indicate that this approach may be superior.

Preliminary results have been obtained estimating duplication using the Headen–Klompmaker–Rust model for cross-pairs,[7] the Rust–Leone–Zimmer model for self-pairs,[18] and the Metheringham beta binomial model for frequency exposure.[15] A test was run on four hundred sample television schedules constructed from SMRB data. In that analysis the estimated duplication approach is clearly better. More work needs to be done before any broad conclusions may be stated with confidence. However if these preliminary results hold up in more extensive testing, they will cast serious doubt on the future prospects of models based on variance estimation.

Mixed-Media Models

It has been assumed thus far that each medium may be examined independently, which is an assumption almost universally employed in practice. However it is common knowledge that media may interact with each other. For example a newspaper ad may work better if an individual has previously been exposed to a companion television ad. Thus it seems reasonable that media models should model more than one medium at once.

Early Efforts

Estimating joint exposure to two or more media has not often been done. The original idea, employed frequently in the original linear programming models in the 1960s, was to pretend that all media vehicles were the same. For example a television ad exposure would be considered the same as a magazine exposure. This assumption is clearly wrong.

Nevertheless to consider the media separately results in considerable practical difficulties. An early attempt to model mixed-media exposure was proposed by Lodish.[14] His method implicitly assumes population homogeneity, and stops short of estimating a joint frequency distribution of exposure.

The Rust–Leone Model

The Rust–Leone model provides an approach to estimating the joint frequency distribution of exposure to a television–magazine advertising schedule.[17] It relaxes the Lodish assumption of population homogeneity. In order to maintain the technical level of the discussion at an acceptable level, and still to provide a modicum of completeness, the original Rust–Leone article is reprinted at the end of this chapter.

Like the Chandon[3] and Leckenby and Kishi[12] models described earlier in the chapter, the Rust–Leone model employs the Dirichlet multinomial distribution (DMD). The general idea is to first estimate the marginal frequency distributions for each of the two media, and then, using estimated intermedia duplication, estimate the full joint frequency distribution of exposure. Thus we would have $f(x_1,x_2)$—the proportion of the population exposed to x_1 television ads and x_2 magazine ads—for every combination of x_1 and x_2.

The television marginal distribution could be obtained using any of the television models discussed earlier (for example, the estimated duplication approach). The magazine marginal distribution could be obtained using any magazine model (such as Chandon's Dirichlet model).

The Rust–Leone method first estimates beta binomial parameters for the marginal distributions, using the method of moments, from

$$\mu = \sum xf(x)$$

$$\sigma^2 = \sum (x - \mu)^2 f(x)$$

This is necessary because the marginal distributions of the DMD are beta binomials. If the marginals were obtained from beta binomials in the first place, then no adjustment is necessary. Otherwise the beta binomial parameters are used to reestimate the marginal distributions.

Intermedia duplications may be obtained as shown in chapter 3. Each individual is assumed to have a probability of exposure to both a typical television ad in the schedule and a typical magazine ad in the schedule, probabilities of exposure to each of the two media alone, and a probability of nonexposure. These four probabilities are assumed to be distributed Dirichlet. This general approach to the Dirichlet parallels Chandon.[3]

The average intermedia duplication is obtained as

$$\mu_3 \doteq \left(\sum\sum k_{jm} r_j r_m\right) / \, n_1 n_2 \qquad (4.18)$$

where k_{jm} is the duplication constant corresponding to the program type of program j and to magazine m; r_j and r_m are the ratings of the program and of the average issue audience of the magazine; n_1 is the number of television shows in the schedule; and n_2 is the number of magazines in the schedule.

Then, given average TV rating μ_{tv}, mean average issue audience μ_{mag}, and marginal distribution parameters α_{tv}, β_{tv}, α_{mag}, and β_{mag}, we may estimate the Dirichlet parameters

$$S = [\mu_{tv}(\alpha_{tv} + \beta_{tv}) + \alpha_{mag}(\alpha_{mag} + \beta_{mag})]/(\mu_{tv} - \mu_{mag})$$
$$A_0 = \mu_0 S$$
$$A_1 = \mu_1 S$$
$$A_2 = \mu_2 S$$
$$A_3 = \mu_3 S$$

The joint frequency distribution is then obtained through an extended enumeration and adjustment procedure which will not be detailed here, but is discussed extensively in the following reprinted article.

The Rust–Leone model is a practical method of estimating joint exposure distributions for television–magazine advertising schedules. To give some idea of the model's accuracy, the average maximum frequency error for the worst case examined was .004. One would expect that because methods now exist for examining two media at once, the model would begin to attain practical acceptance. One would also anticipate considerable further progress among researchers in the area.

Conclusion

The most striking conclusion is that estimating frequency of exposure is a deceptively difficult area of research. Even the best models proposed have substantial room for improvement. It is also clear after twenty-five years of research in the area that better models will result only from the best efforts of the best applied statisticians. It is a problem that cries out for an appealing general solution, but such a solution has not been achieved.

Among the best models requiring duplications, there is no clear winner. The drawbacks of the popular beta binomial distribution are well documented. Yet its successors are not clearly superior. Greene's beta matrix method has undesirable theoretical properties, the simulation models require a prohibitive amount of computation, and the Dirichlet models are limited to situations in which there are an equal number of insertions in each vehicle.

Among the models not requiring duplications, the Rust–Klompmaker television model appears to be the best. The Leckenby–Rice model also has performed well on a limited data set, but theoretical considerations cast doubt on whether it would perform well in general. All of the above models may prove to be inferior to the estimated duplications method, if preliminary results hold up. This approach requires the estimation of the duplications, which are then input to a frequency model (such as Metheringham) to estimate the frequency distribution of exposure.

There has been little work done in mixed-media models. Only the Rust–Leone model exists for estimating intermedia exposure for television–magazine schedules.

References

1. David A. Aaker, "ADMOD: An Advertising Decision Model," *Journal of Marketing Research* (February 1975):37–45.

2. Ramaiya Balachandra, *Media Selection and Advertising Scheduling Strategy,* doctoral dissertation (New York: Columbia University, 1975).

3. Jean–Louis Chandon, *A Comparative Study of Media Exposure Models,* doctoral dissertation (Evanston, Ill.: Northwestern University, 1976).

4. Dennis H. Gensch, "A Computer Simulation Model for Selecting Advertising Schedules," *Journal of Marketing Research* (May 1969):203–14.

5. Jerome D. Greene and J.S. Stock, *Advertising Reach and Frequency in Magazines* (New York: Marketmath and Reader's Digest Association, 1967).

6. Bernard Guggenheim, "Advertising Media Planning and Evaluation: Current Research Issues" in *Current Issues and Research in Advertising,* vol. 2, ed. James H. Leigh and Claude R. Martin (Ann Arbor: University of Michigan, 1984), 19–38.

7. Robert S. Headen, Jay E. Klompmaker, and Roland T. Rust, "The Duplication of Viewing Law and Television Media Schedule Evaluation," *Journal of Marketing Research* (August 1979):333–40.

8. Robert S. Headen, Jay E. Klompmaker, and Jesse E. Teel, "Predicting Audience Exposure to Spot TV Advertising Schedules," *Journal of Marketing Research* (February 1977):1–9.

9. Pierre Hofmans, "Measuring the Cumulative Net Coverage of any Combination of Media," *Journal of Marketing Research* (August 1966):269–78.

10. Herbert E. Krugman, "Why Three Exposures May Be Enough," *Journal of Advertising Research* (December 1972):11–14.

11. John D. Leckenby and Shizue Kishi, "How Media Directors View Reach/Frequency Estimation," *Journal of Advertising Research* (June–July 1982):64–69.

12. John D. Leckenby and Shizue Kishi, "The Dirichlet Multinomial Distribution as a Magazine Exposure Model," *Journal of Marketing Research* (February 1984):100–6.

13. John D. Leckenby and Marshall D. Rice, "A Beta Binomial Network TV Exposure Model Using Limited Data," *Journal of Advertising* 3 (1985):25–31.

14. Leonard M. Lodish, "Exposure Interactions among Media Schedules," *Journal of Advertising Research* (April 1973):31–34.

15. Richard A. Metheringham, "Measuring the Net Cumulative Coverage of a Print Campaign," *Journal of Advertising Research* (December 1964):23–28.

16. Roland T. Rust and Jay E. Klompmaker, "Improving the Estimation Procedure for the Beta Binomial TV Exposure Model," *Journal of Marketing Research* (November 1981):442–48.

17. Roland T. Rust and Robert P. Leone, "The Mixed Media Dirichlet Multinomial Distribution: A Model for Evaluating Television–Magazine Advertising Schedules," *Journal of Marketing Research* (February 1984):89–99.

18. Roland T. Rust, Robert P. Leone, and Mary R. Zimmer, "Estimating the Duplicated Audience of Media Vehicles in National Advertising Schedules," working paper, University of Texas at Austin.

19. Darius J. Sabavala and Donald G. Morrison, "A Nonstationary Model of Binary Choice Applied to Media Exposure," *Management Science* (June 1981), 637–57.

20. Robert J. Schreiber, "Instability in Media Exposure Habits," *Journal of Advertising Research* (April 1974):13–17.

21. Simmons Media Studies, *Technical Guide: 1977/1978 Study of Selective Markets and the Media Reaching Them* (New York: Simmons Media Studies, 1978).

Appendix 4A: The Mixed–Media Dirichlet Multinomial Distribution: A Model for Evaluating Television–Magazine Advertising Schedules

Roland T. Rust
Robert P. Leone

In recent years, because of increased costs and competition, companies have begun to give more attention to achieving higher levels of efficiency and effectiveness in resource allocation. Many companies can achieve dramatic savings from more efficient advertising expenditures. For example, if Procter & Gamble could reduce its network television advertising budget by 1 percent with no loss in sales or market share, the result would be a saving of $3.61 million (*Advertising Age* 1982).

As most national advertisers use advertising campaigns that include both television and magazines, the allocation question involves determining not only the total budget, but also the proportion of that budget to be spent in each medium, because various proportions of the same total dollar figure would yield significantly different results. A typical example is American Airlines, which in 1980 spent $28.5 million on television advertising and $9.7 million on magazine advertising. The corresponding advertising schedules may be termed "mixed-media advertising schedules," because advertising dollars must be allocated to more than one medium.

Many proposed media-selection models that are purported to accommodate the mixed-media schedule selection problem simply lump the vehicles in the various media together in such a way that exposure to a television ad is assumed to be equivalent to exposure to a magazine ad (Srinivasan 1976; Zufryden 1973). Other models involve the assumption that the effectiveness

---

Reprinted by permission, "The Mixed-Media Dirichlet Multinomial Distribution: A Model for Evaluating Television–Magazine Advertising Schedules," Roland T. Rust and Robert P. Leone, *Journal of Marketing Research* vol. XXI (February 1984), 89–99.

The authors thank John D. Leckenby and Shizue Kishi for providing software used for the magazine exposure estimation component of the model, and also Simmons Market Research Bureau, Inc. for providing data used in the study.

of ads in various media differs quantitatively but not qualitatively. (For example, the weights might be such that one television exposure is twice as effective as one magazine exposure.) This theoretical assumption, embodied in media weights and appropriateness weights (Aaker 1975; Aaker and Brown 1972; Bass and Lonsdale 1966; Gensch 1969, 1970; Little and Lodish 1969) has been found to be unrealistic; research by Sperry (1973) and others on brain activity has led media theorists to hypothesize qualitative differences in cognitive response to the various advertising media (Barksdale and Klompmaker 1979; Hansen 1981; Krugman 1977). Magazines and television have been shown to generate different types of brain activity (Krugman 1971; Weinstein, Appel, and Weinstein 1980). The differences in brain activity have been linked theoretically to differential response to visual and verbal stimuli (Krugman 1980a, b). These qualitative differences, if real, imply that the traditional approaches may be inadequate in modeling response to mixed-media advertising schedules and could lead to incorrect budget allocation decisions.

Print and broadcast media have been found to differ in effectiveness in terms of awareness, image, and perceived advantages of a product (Hugues 1975). Media differences in communication effectiveness (Grass and Wallace 1974), effect on market share (Prasad and Ring 1976; Sexton 1970), creation of cognitive connections (Bogart, Tolley, and Orenstein; Krugman 1966–67), and information source use patterns (Hirschman and Mills 1980; Larkin 1972) also have been observed. In addition, a general difference between television and magazines in conditioned arousal response to the media themselves may exist (Rossiter 1980), which would imply that qualitative media differences would exist regardless of message content.

As might be expected, past research also shows that response to mixed-media advertising may involve complex interactive effects. For example, when television advertising is used to support a print campaign, the combined effect has been found to be larger than the effect of the two media separately (Jain 1975). Interactive effects also have been found between product, message, and medium (Buchanan 1964; McConnell 1970).

Because considerable theory and empirical evidence suggest a qualitative difference in response to television and magazine advertising, and that this response may involve complex interactions, any model estimating exposure to mixed-media advertising schedules that does not consider a joint distribution of exposure may be misspecified. It is therefore surprising that very little research has been done on estimating joint exposure to a mixed-media advertising schedule. Lodish (1973) proposed a method of estimating the exposure interactions between two media schedules (which might represent two media). The method implicitly assumes population homogeneity, but stops short of estimating a joint distribution of exposure.

Though little has been done on estimating joint exposure to mixed-media schedules, considerable work has been done on the estimation of exposure to television or magazine advertising schedules individually. Most modern exposure models are based on either the beta distribution or its multivariate analog, the Dirichlet distribution. Each of these distributions allows the modeling of heterogeneity in exposure probability across the population.

The beta binomial distribution (BBD) is a compound distribution which estimates a frequency distribution of exposure (proportion of people exposed zero, one, two times, etc.) from the beta distribution. First widely used in the 1960s (Greene and Stock 1967), the BBD has been adapted to fit various circumstances and assumptions such as nonstationarity (Sabavala and Morrison 1981; Schreiber 1974).

Magazine models using the BBD date back to the procedure proposed by Metheringham (1964). The Dirichlet multinomial distribution (DMD), a multivariate extension of the BBD, was found by Chandon (1976) to be empirically superior to the BBD magazine model. Leckenby and Kishi (1982b) recently have extended the DMD magazine distribution by incorporating approximations first derived by Hofmans (1966). Their empirical tests reconfirmed the DMD's superiority over the BBD magazine models.

The magazine BBD and DMD models require pair-wise duplication data. Television exposure models differ from magazine models in that these duplication data are not generally available as inputs. The simple binomial model (Balachandra 1975; Aaker 1975) has been used, but a better approach appears to be the creative estimation of a BBD (Headen, Klompmaker, and Teel 1977). In this approach, available information about the characteristics of the television schedule (such as number of networks used, number of programs used, average rating, etc.) is a proxy for duplication in estimating the parameters of the model. An extension of this model recently has been proposed (Rust and Klompmaker 1981).

In the next section we propose a model of joint exposure to a mixed-media advertising schedule. We then develop alternative models based on other plausible theoretical assumptions. A large-sample cross-validated empirical test is presented next, and the performance of the proposed model is compared with that of the alternative models. After a discussion of the results of the empirical test, we examine the implications of the findings to the organization of the media planning function.

The Model

Many good models are available for estimating the marginal distributions of exposure to the respective television and magazine subschedules of a mixed-media advertising schedule. What is needed is a method of combining these marginal distributions, using as additional input the estimated intermedia duplications, into a full joint distribution of exposure.

We present the mixed-media Dirichlet multinomial distribution

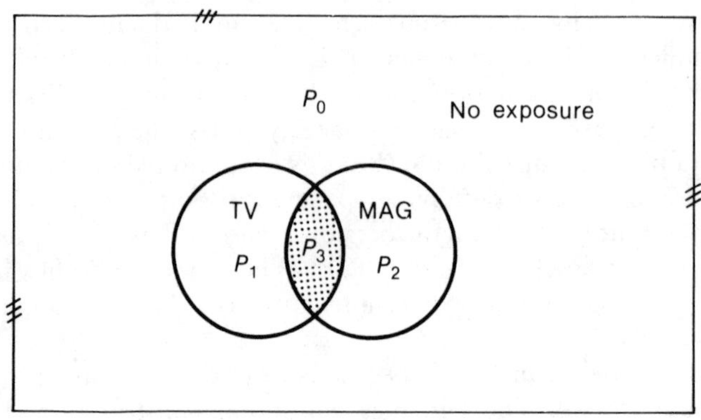

$\Sigma p_i = 1$ for each individual, p distributed Dirichlet over the population.

Figure 4A–1. Dirichlet Exposure Probabilities

(MMDMD) model, which employs an exposure model based on the Dirichlet distribution. The Dirichlet has been applied widely in brand choice studies (such as Jeuland, Bass, and Wright 1980; Kalwani 1980; Shoemaker et al. 1977), but media applications have been few. Chandon (1976) used the Dirichlet to model exposure involving only magazines and his model has been tested further on magazines. The authors are unaware of any application of the Dirichlet to mixed-media exposure.

Employing the same vehicle homogeneity assumption typically made for beta binomial exposure models[1] (Chandon 1976; Headen, Klompmaker, and Teel 1977; Metheringham 1964), we assume each individual has a probability P_{tv} of viewing a typical television show in the schedule, a probability P_{mag} of reading a typical magazine issue in the schedule, and a probability P_3 of both seeing the television show *and* reading the magazine issue. Defining $P_1 = P_{tv} - P_3$ (probability of exclusive exposure to the television show), $P_2 = P_{mag} - P_3$ (probability of exclusive exposure to the magazine issue), and $P_0 = 1 - P_2 - P_3$ (probability of nonexposure to both), we may view the probability events involved with exposure to a television show and magazine issue as disjoint (Chandon 1976), and assume the probabilities to be Dirichlet distributed over the population. The probabilities of exposure to each medium then can be calculated by using the inclusion/exclusion principle (Feller 1969, p. 106; Kwerel 1968). Figure 4A–1 is a diagrammatic representation.

Estimation of the Model

We assume as input to the model marginal distributions of exposure $M_1(Z_1)(Z_1 = 0, \ldots, n_1)$ for television and $M_2(Z_2)(Z_2 = 0, \ldots, n_2)$ for magazines given that the mixed-media advertising schedule consists of single insertions in n_1 television shows and n_2 magazine issues. These marginal distributions can be estimated by any of the many available methods discussed before.

Because the Dirichlet assumes BBD marginal distributions, the first step is to approximate the marginal distributions M_1 and M_2 by BBD marginals M_1^* and M_2^*. These fits can be accomplished easily by the method of moments (Chandon 1976). The BBD approximation is only an intermediate step. The original marginals, no matter how they have been estimated, are preserved in the final joint frequency distribution. If BBDs are used originally to estimate marginals M_1 and M_2, which frequently may be the case because of the widespread use of the BBD in media models, no approximation is necessary and marginals M_1 and M_2 can be used directly as the marginals of the Dirichlet.

The television BBD marginal distribution M_1 is characterized by beta parameters α_1 and β_1, and the number of television ads, n_1; the magazine BBD marginal distribution M_2^* is characterized by α_2, β_2, and n_2. The mean television audience is

$$\mu_{tv} = \alpha_1 / (\alpha_1 + \beta_1) \tag{4A–1}$$

and the mean magazine audience is

$$\mu_{mag} = \alpha_2 / (\alpha_2 + \beta_2). \tag{4A–2}$$

Estimating Intermediate Duplication

With the marginal distributions, the average intermedia duplication, μ_3 (corresponding to probability P_3 in figure 4A–1), supplies the remaining information necessary to estimate the parameters of the Dirichlet distribution. Little work has been done in estimating audience duplication between media vehicles in different media. Also, as magazine duplications are readily available, little work has been done on estimating pairwise magazine duplication. Because television duplications are rarely reported, however, several estimation methods are available for predicting the duplication of television programs. Goodhardt and Ehrenberg (1969) produced a simple method, based on the observation that duplication tends to be proportional to the product of the audience sizes. Sabavala and Morrison (1977) explored duplication in terms of the properties of the BBD, and recent work (Headen, Klompmaker, and Rust 1979; Rust, Klompmaker, and Headen 1981) has sought to revitalize the Goodhardt–Ehrenberg method through the utilization of program characteristics.

We use a variant of the Goodhardt–Ehrenberg method to estimate intermedia duplication. Though duplications between particular magazines and particular television programs generally will not be known because of the transitory nature of television programming, historical data (such as Simmons) are available on the duplications between particular magazines and program types. The program types used for this estimation are serial drama, action drama, psychological drama, game show, talk or variety show, movie, news, and comedy. These program types are used because they have been shown to improve significantly the estimation of television audience duplication (Headen, Klompmaker, and Rust 1979).

Using the Goodhardt–Ehrenberg approach, we estimate duplicated audience of a television program i and a magazine m as

$$\hat{r}_{im} = k_{jm} r_i r_m \tag{4A–3}$$

where r_i is the audience proportion for television program i, r_m is the audience proportion for magazine m, and k_{jm} is the duplication "constant" corresponding to magazine m and program type j (for a specific television program i).

To estimate the duplication, the value of k_{jm} is required. Analogous to previous results (Rust, Klompmaker, and Headen 1981), a least squares estimate for k_{jm} is

$$\hat{k}_{jm} = \left[\sum_{i \epsilon j}\sum_{m}(r_i r_m r_{im})\right] / \left[\sum_{i \epsilon j}\sum_{m}(r_i^2 r_m^2)\right]. \tag{4A–4}$$

This estimation is performed on a large set of historical data.

Given the duplication constants for combinations of magazines and program types, along with the audience proportions for the television programs and magazines in the schedule, we now can obtain the parameters of the Dirichlet. The average intermedia duplication μ_3, corresponding to probability P_3 in figure 4A–1, can be estimated as

$$\mu_3 = \left[\sum_{i}\sum_{m}\hat{k}_{jm} r_i r_m\right] / n_1 n_2 \tag{4A–5}$$

where j is the program type corresponding to program i.

The other Dirichlet means now can be estimated

$$\hat{\mu}_1 = \mu_{tv} - \hat{\mu}_3$$

$$\hat{\mu}_2 = \mu_{mag} - \hat{\mu}_3$$

$$\hat{\mu}_0 = 1 - \hat{\mu}_1 - \hat{\mu}_2 - \hat{\mu}_3$$

The parameters of the Dirichlet can be obtained by multiplying the means by a factor of S, a weighted average of the sum of the BBD marginal distribution parameters (Chandon 1976).

$$S = [\mu_{tv}(\alpha_1 + \beta_1) + \mu_{mag}(\alpha_2 + \beta_2)]/(\mu_{tv} - \mu_{mag}) \tag{4A–6}$$

$$A_0 = \hat{\mu}_0 S$$

$$A_1 = \hat{\mu}_1 S$$

$$A_2 = \hat{\mu}_2 S$$

$$A_3 = \hat{\mu}_3 S$$

The distribution across the population of the probabilities diagrammed in figure 4A–1 is the following Dirichlet distribution.

$$D(P_0, P_1, P_2, P_3) = \Gamma(A_0 + A_1 + A_2 + A_3) \cdot P_0^{A_0 - 1} \cdot P_1^{A_1 - 1} P_2^{A_2 - 1} P_3^{A_3 - 1}$$

$$\cdot [\Gamma(A_0)\Gamma(A_1)\Gamma(A_2)\Gamma(A_3)]^{-1}$$

$$0 \leq P_i \leq 1, \sum P_1 = 1 \qquad i = 0, 1, 2, 3, \tag{4A–7}$$

where Γ denotes the gamma function.

The Dirichlet distribution can be used to generate a full joint exposure distribution by compounding with the multinomial distribution. The resulting compound distribution, termed the "Dirichlet multinomial distribution" (DMD), has been studied extensively in the literature (Chandon 1976; Kalwani 1980; Johnson and Kotz 1969, 1972).

Chandon (1976) showed how the exposure to a schedule consisting of equal numbers of insertions in each of two magazines could be described as repeated trials from a sample space similar to that in figure 4A–1.[2] Mixed-media exposure is analogous, the two media corresponding to the two magazines in the Chandon application.

When the DMD is applied to the mixed-media exposure problem by the formulation we present, the numbers of insertions in the two media must be equal. This requirement results from the mathematical form of the DMD. The use of dummy insertions in the medium that is used less overcomes this apparent limitation. As an example, let us assume five television insertions and three magazine insertions are used in an advertising schedule. Two dummy magazine insertions are added so the DMD can be used. The result will be that more magazine exposures than we should expect will be estimated in the joint frequency distribution. The results of the DMD therefore must be adjusted statistically, as discussed by Greene and Stock (1967).

Including the dummy insertions, the estimated distribution of the four exposure events is

$$P(k_0, k_1, k_2, k_3) = \frac{n!}{\Pi(k_i!)} \cdot \frac{\Gamma(\Sigma A_i)}{\Pi(\Gamma(A_i))} \cdot \frac{\Pi(\Gamma(k_i + A_i))}{\Gamma(n + \Sigma A_i)}. \tag{4A–8}$$

The number k_1 signifies the number of exposures[3] exclusive to television, k_2 signifies the number of exposures exclusive to magazine, and k_3 signifies the number of exposures to both television and magazine. Thus, the total number of television exposures is $k_1 + k_3$, and the total number of magazine exposures is $k_2 + k_3$. The ensuing joint distribution of exposure (still reflecting the dummy ads) is

$$g(y_1,y_2) = \sum_A P(k_0,k_1,k_2,k_3) \tag{4A–9}$$

where

$$A = \{k_0,k_1,k_2,k_3 \mid k_1 + k_3 = y_1; k_2 + k_3 = y_2\}.$$

The preceding joint distribution must be adjusted to remove the effect of the dummy ads. This step is accomplished using the hypergeometric distribution. As an example of the method of adjustment, let us suppose that $n, > n_2$. In other words, there were more television ads than magazine ads, and therefore magazine dummy ads were added. We would have

$$f^*(x_1,x_2) = \frac{\binom{n_2}{x_2}\binom{n - n_2}{y_2 - x_2}}{\binom{n}{y_2}} \cdot g(y_1,y_2) \tag{4A–10}$$

where f^* is the DMD joint distribution estimate with dummy ads removed, x_1 is the number of television exposures, x_2 is the number of magazine exposures, and n is the larger of the number of insertions.

Another possible problem is that original marginal distributions M_1 and M_2, used as input to the procedure, in general will not be equal to marginal distributions M_1^* and M_2^* obtained from the DMD. This difference may be a problem when the input marginals are more accurate than their BBD approximations. In this case, the joint distribution $f^*(x_1,x_2)$ can be adjusted by Deming's procedure (Deming and Stephan 1940) to conform to the original marginals, producing the final estimated joint frequency distribution $\hat{f}(x_1,x_2)$. The magnitude of the adjustment is usually small.

Alternative Models

The MMDMD model proceeds from two fundamental assumptions: (1) exposure to a television ad has a different effect than exposure to a magazine ad and (2) the effects of intermedia duplication necessitate the estimation of a joint frequency distribution of exposure. In this section we develop alternative models which result from relaxing the assumptions underlying MMDMD.

The Univariate DMD Model

If assumption 1 is relaxed but assumption 2 is retained, the options in both media may be combined as though only one medium were involved. Given that the television pairwise duplications are first estimated, an existing magazine exposure estimation model can be used.

Although the Leckenby–Kishi (1982b) Dirichlet models were not designed for mixed-media applications, one of them can be extended to the mixed-media case if assumption 1 is relaxed. To apply this model, we first estimate television duplications using the methods in the preceding section. A univariate frequency distribution of exposure then is estimated for the combined television–magazine schedule by means of the Leckenby–Kishi DMDH model.[4] This model is used as one of the alternatives because it is the magazine exposure model that has obtained the best empirical results (Leckenby and Kishi 1982b) without sacrificing theoretical justification.

The Independent Joint Model (IJM)

If assumption 1 is retained but assumption 2 is relaxed, each medium can be estimated separately. Then, if consideration of indermedia duplication is unnecessary, the two marginals can be multiplied together as though they were statistically independent to produce a joint frequency distribution.

To operationalize these assumptions, we use the Leckenby–Kishi DMDH model to estimate the magazine exposure distribution, again because this is probably the best available magazine exposure method. The television exposure distribution is estimated by the best published BBD television exposure method (Rust and Klompmaker 1981). We then multiply out the joint frequency distribution, assuming independence of the two marginal distributions.

Empirical Test

Many media models involve the simplifying assumption that an exposure to one medium is the same as an exposure to another. If this is true, the univariate DMD model should result in good predictions of response to an advertising schedule. If media planning is appropriately done separately for television and magazines, the independent joint model (IJM) should be adequate. It should result in good predictions of both the joint frequency distribution of exposure and the ensuing response to the schedule. We tested the relative performance of the three models for a large number of schedules, using several different response assumptions. The predicted exposure distributions were compared with exposures obtained in a large-sample diary study of media exposure.

Data

The data used to test the models were provided by the Simmons Market Research Bureau and are from their 1977–78 report (Simmons 1978a, b). The Simmons respondents were selected by means of a multistage area cluster sample. Joint data on television viewing and magazine readership were collected from 5,652 respondents in a six-week period from October 9 to November 19, 1977. The 5,652 respondents were a subsample of 15,003 original respondents, all of whom answered questionnaires about demographic characteristics, product usage, and media use. Our media exposure tabulations are based on the television subsample.

Response Assumptions

Sixteen sets of response assumptions are used in the analysis. They arise from two possible shapes of the advertising response function, whether response was interactive or additive between the two media, and four relative effectiveness weights[5] for the two media. Though many other sets of response assumptions might have been constructed, we believe a wide range of current beliefs about advertising response is encompassed by these sixteen possibilities.

There is considerable controversy as to whether a threshold number of exposures is necessary to stimulate response effectively (Krugman 1972) or whether exposures undergo immediate diminishing returns (Simon and Arndt 1980). Each of these assumptions is investigated in our analysis. There is evidence that advertising campaigns in two media may have an interactive effect. We consider both interactive and noninteractive response. Also, exposures in the two media may not carry the same weight. The following response functions incorporate the preceding response assumptions.

The first response function is the *DN* (diminishing returns, noninteractive) function

$$RESP(XTV, XMAG) = (W1(XTV^{.5})) + (XMAG^{.5}) \quad (4A\text{–}11)$$

where *RESP* is response (sales, recall, attendance, or some other effectiveness criterion), W1 is a weight (lower .5, equal 1, higher 2, or much higher 5) corresponding to the relative effectiveness of television in comparison with magazines, *XTV* is the number of television exposures, and *XMAG* is the number of magazine exposures. The exponent .5 was chosen because it produces a recognizable diminishing returns shape for the response function, and empirical results have shown that it has approximated advertising response as well (Rust 1979).

The second response function is the *DI* (diminishing returns, interactive) function

$$RESP(XTV, XMAG) = ((XTV^{W1})(XMAG^{.5})).$$

The third response function is the *TN* (threshold, noninteractive) function

$$RESP(XTV, XMAG) = RTV(XTV) + RMAG(XMAG)$$

where *RTV* is the response due to television, *RMAG* is the response due to magazines, and

$$RTV(XTV) = W2 \text{ if } XTV \geq 2$$

$$RMAG(XMAG) = 2 \text{ if } XMAG \geq 2$$

where *W*2 is a relative media effectiveness weight (lower 1, equal 2, higher 4, or much higher 10).

The fourth response function is the *TI* (threshold, interactive) function

$$RESP(XTV, XMAG) = 1 \text{ if } XTV \geq 2 \text{ and } XMAG \geq W3$$

where *W*3 is the media effectiveness weight (lower 1, equal 2, higher 3, or much higher 4).

Response for the four error measures is scale-dependent and is not comparable across error measures. For this reason, proportion error statistics (which are independent of scale used) are employed in the discussion of error statistics.

Though manipulation of these response assumptions clearly is not exhaustive, it provides for an extensive comparison of the models' abilities to fit the data because their performances are measured under various circumstances. It also provides a framework for analyzing the performances of the models through an analysis of variance.

Error Criteria

For each set of response assumptions, the three models were compared on the basis of several goodness-of-fit measures. The primary measure was the absolute difference between the predicted total response and the total response inferred from the actual observed joint frequency distribution. This error for each test schedule was calculated as

$$ERROR = |\text{predicted response} - \text{actual response}| / \text{actual response} \qquad (4A\text{–}12)$$

where

$$\text{predicted response} = \sum_{XTV} \sum_{XMAG} \hat{f}(XTV, XMAG) RESP(XTV, XMAG),$$

$$\text{actual response} = \sum_{XTV} \sum_{XMAG} f(XTV, XMAG) RESP(XTV, XMAG),$$

and f is the actual observed joint frequency distribution, $\hat{f}$ is the estimated distribution, and *RESP* is response as defined previously.

Because the univariate DMD model does not produce a joint frequency distribution comparable to those used to compute *ERROR,* we used an alternative method to estimate response for that model. In order not to bias against the univariate model, we obtained the expected univariate response function from the joint response function and the observed joint frequency distributions for the 660 test schedules.

$$R(XTOT) = \sum_{i=1}^{660} \sum_{XTV=0}^{XTOT} f_i(XTV, XTOT - XTV) \; RESP(XTV, XTOT - XTV) \Big/ \sum_{i=1}^{660} \sum_{XTV=0}^{XTOT} f_i(XTV, XTOT - XTV) \qquad (4A\text{–}13)$$

where R is the expected univariate response function, f_i is the observed joint frequency distribution from schedule i, and $XTOT$ is the total of the television exposures plus the magazine exposures. Each univariate exposure level corresponds to the one or more cells in the joint frequency distribution. The univariate response then is the weighted sum of the response over those corresponding cells. Equation 4A–13 calculates these weighted sums by determining the empirically correct[6] weights from the observed data.

Given the estimated univariate frequency distribution *FU* obtained by using the univariate DMD model and the univariate response function *R,* we can compute the predicted response.

$$\text{predicted response} = \sum_{XTOT} FU(XTOT) R(XTOT)$$

Three additional error measures were used to evaluate the joint frequency distribution estimation accuracy of both MMDMD and the independent joint model—*SSQ,* the sum of square frequency error over the cells; *MAX,* the maximum frequency error over the cells; and AVABS, the average absolute frequency error across the cells.

$$SSQ = \sum_{XTV} \sum_{XMAG} (\hat{f}(XTV, XMAG) - f(XTV, XMAG))^2 \quad (4A\text{–}14)$$

$$MAX = \max_{XTV,\ XMAG} |\hat{f}(XTV, XMAG) - f(XTV, XMAG)| \quad (4A\text{–}15)$$

$$AVABS = \Big(\sum_{XTV} \sum_{XMAG} |\hat{f}(XTV, XMAG) - f(XTV, XMAG)|\Big) / (NTV - NMAG) \quad (4A\text{–}16)$$

Research Design

A random sample of 600 mixed-media schedules was drawn from the magazine and television vehicles measured in the Simmons data to serve as the primary test data for the three models being compared. Each of the schedules had ten total "insertions." ("Insertions" here refers to magazine insertions plus television spots.) The actual joint frequency distributions were tabulated directly from the Simmons data. The estimation methods employed only the television ratings, magazine audiences, and magazine pairwise duplications—data that are readily available to media planners. The number of television spots (NTV) was varied, with 200 scheduled each for $NTV = 3, 5,$ and 7.

As a further test of predictive validity, 60 schedules constructed to target particular segments were produced. The first 24 schedules were assembled from media vehicles yielding a low cost per thousand for a demographic target segment. Three schedules (with $NTV = 3, 5,$ and 7) were produced for each of eight demographic segments differing by age, sex, and education. The final 36 schedules were built from media vehicles yielding a low cost per thousand for the users of a particular product. Again three schedules (with $NTV = 3, 5,$ and 7) were produced for each of 12 consumer products ranging from nondurables to durables. The actual exposure distributions for these schedules also were tabulated directly from the Simmons data to test the accuracy of the estimation methods. One would expect schedules targeted to a particular segment to produce high duplication, thus making the exposure-modeling task more challenging.

Results and Discussion

The performance of MMDMD and the two alternative models in estimating exposure is summarized in table 4A–1. The performance of MMDMD is very good. For the random schedules, the average estimation error per cell is only

Table 4A–1
Mean Errors in Estimating Exposures

		Effective Response Errors				*Unadjusted Errors*		
Schedule Basis	*Model*	*DN*	*DI*	*TN*	*TI*	*SSQ*[a]	*MAX*[a]	*AVABS*[a]
Random	MMDMD	.005	.106	.019	.043	.006	.384	.079
	IJM	.020	.124	.100	.451	.064	1.409	.193
	Univariate	.123	.475	.281	.805	—	—	—
Demographic segment	MMDMD	.022	.233	.038	.286	.006	.435	.089
	IJM	1.204	2.959	.637	1.073	14.261	28.580	2.841
	Univariate	1.302	2.794	1.078	3.107	—	—	—
Product usage segment	MMDMD	.018	.217	.044	.334	.004	.322	.065
	IJM	.768	1.809	.405	.890	5.225	16.053	1.532
	Univariate	.825	1.903	.755	1.325	—	—	—

[a]Numbers × 10^{-2}.

.0008 and the average maximum cell error per schedule is only .0038. The proportion error statistics appear somewhat worse, but closer inspection indicates that the magnitude of the average proportion errors may be misleading because they are largely due to the effect of the sparse cells artificially inflating the error statistics. In all error categories MMDMD has the smallest error. The IJM error is the next smallest in every case whereas the univariate model's performance is poor in comparison with that of both MMDMD and the IJM.

Table 4A–1 also shows that for the demographic and product usage segments MMDMD's performance is better than that of the univariate model and the IJM across all error categories. Also, though the performance of MMDMD decreases somewhat for these target segment schedules, the performance of the univariate and IJM models deteriorate dramatically. This finding is most likely due to the high television audience–magazine readership overlaps which inevitably occur in a skillful media plan.

The statistical significance of the difference for the random schedules is reported in table 4A–2. MMDMD is significantly better than the IJM model in every case at the .001 level. Given the large sample size, the statistical significance of the differences is not surprising. However, the practical significance of the differences in error between alternatives should not be underestimated. Referring again to Procter & Gamble's annual network television–magazine advertising budget of $398 million (*Advertising Age* 1982) we find that the error difference between MMDMD and IJM from the response assumption (*DN*) with the *smallest* error difference amounts to $5.97 million annually. The response assumption (*TN*) with the *largest* error difference results in an error magnitude of $32.2 million.

The comparative performance of the models also is evaluated by calcu-

Table 4A–2
Significance of the Difference in Exposure Estimation Accuracy between MMDMD and IJM for the 600 Random Schedules

Error Measure	*Difference*	*t*	*Significance*
ERROR			
DN	1.51[a]	36.16	.001
DI	1.79[a]	13.51	.001
TN	8.14[a]	31.66	.001
TI	4.73[a]	3.36	.001
SSQ	.60[b]	9.34	.001
MAX	10.30[b]	41.02	.001
AVABS	1.10[b]	33.85	.001

[a]Numbers × 10^{-2}.
[b]Numbers × 10^{-3}.

Table 4A–3
Proportion of Schedules in Which MMDMD Outperformed IJM with Respect to ERROR

		TV Weight Relative to Magazine Weight				
Schedule Basis	*Response*	*ALL*	*Lowest*	*Equal*	*Higher*	*Much Higher*
Random	*DN*	.85	.88	.86	.84	.84
	DI	.64	.63	.63	.66	.64
	TN	.88	.83	.87	.90	.91
	TI	.59	.67	.53	.53	.61
Demographic	*DN*	.99	.96	1.00	1.00	1.00
	DI	1.00	1.00	1.00	1.00	1.00
	TN	.91	.88	.75	1.00	1.00
	TI	.86	.88	1.00	.77	.78
Product usage	*DN*	1.00	1.00	1.00	1.00	1.00
	DI	.85	1.00	1.00	1.00	1.00
	TN	.94	.94	.92	.94	.94
	TI	.67	.67	.74	.63	.66

lating the proportion of schedules in which MMDMD outperforms an alternative model. Table 4A–3 shows MMDMD's dominance over IJM. When error is averaged over all television effectiveness weights considered, MMDMD is better for each response assumption at the .01 level. This table shows MMDMD's increasing dominance for the two target segment schedules that are based on demographic data and product usage.

MMDMD's advantage is smaller for both interactive response cases, but the reason for this finding is unclear. Perhaps it is because the multiplicative model used to calculate the *DI* response makes the predicted response more sensitive to errors in estimating exposure, thus making it difficult to obtain a very good response estimate regardless of the model used. Also, in the *TI* case, the fact that only a few cells in the joint frequency distribution contribute to response could lead to more erratic performance. These interpretations are consistent with the error magnitudes observed in table 4A–1.

Table 4A–3 also shows the superiority of MMDMD as we look across television effectiveness weights. Further evidence of MMDMD's consistency is given in table 4A–4, which evaluates average response error across response functions and television effectiveness weights. In addition, this table illustrates the catastrophic levels of error that may arise from the univariate model—several errors are in excess of 200 percent.

MMDMD's degree of advantage is not uniform across the media composition (number of TV ads, *NTV*, in the schedule), response assumption (*RSP*), and the television effectiveness weight (*WGT*). An overall ANOVA using these three variables to decompose the extent of MMDMD's advantage over its alternatives could not be run because of the unavoidable noncomparability of television effectiveness weight which was operationalized differently for each response assumption. However, we were able to construct such an ANOVA to explain MMDMD's advantage over the univariate model, using *NTV* and *RSP* as independent variables and aggregating across all weight levels. *NTV* and *RSP* were found to be significant, largely because of the sample size, but the proportion of variance they explain is small. However, in terms of practical significance, MMDMD's advantage over the univariate model is fairly uniform. Similar results were obtained from comparison of MMDMD with the IJM.

ANOVAs also were run for each response case to assess the effect of *NTV* and television weight (*WGT*) on each model's performance. The only case in which MMDMD did not significantly outperform the alternatives was the decreasing returns–interactive (*DI*) case where *WGT* was not significant. MMDMD always performed better than the alternatives when the television effectiveness weight was different from the magazine weight.

The general conclusion arising from the analysis is that MMDMD, which actively models joint exposure to a mixed-media advertising schedule using television and magazines, is preferable to both alternative models which represent procedures currently used. MMDMD's advantage is consistent across response assumptions, media weights, and media composition of the schedule.

Of perhaps even greater importance is the finding that MMDMD is much more robust to assumptions about these factors. MMDMD performed better for all response assumptions tested. Its advantage increased as the number of television ads became greater or fewer than average, and as media effectiveness weights became dissimilar.

Implications for Media Planning

Considerable cumulative evidence indicates important qualitative differences between television ad exposures and magazine ad exposures. This conclusion is supported both by psychological theories of cognitive response and brain function and by a wealth of empirical data. Our analysis postulates different media effectiveness weights, types of response, and degrees of interaction. It also considers the effect of varying the media composition of the schedule and the logic upon which the schedule is constructed.

The MMDMD model enables a media planner to model joint exposure to an advertising schedule containing both television and magazine ads. Great flexibility is maintained, permitting the application of response assumptions that may represent any degree of interaction between the media

Table 4A–4
Average *ERROR* Across Schedules by Response Function and TV Weight

Schedule Basis	*TV Weight Relative to Magazine Weight*	*Model*	*Response*			
			DN	*DI*	*TN*	*TI*
Random	Lower	MMDMD	.005	.099	.020	.458
		IJM	.024	.118	.070	.701
		Univariate	.107	.491	.345	.922
	Equal	MMDMD	.005	.101	.019	.815
		IJM	.021	.118	.085	.826
		Univariate	.020	.482	.207	1.226
	Higher	MMDMD	.005	.106	.018	.590
		IJM	.018	.122	.105	.710
		Univariate	.118	.466	.187	2.752
	Much higher	MMDMD	.004	.117	.018	.606
		IJM	.017	.138	.140	.767
		Univariate	.248	.462	.386	4.798
Demographic	Lower	MMDMD	.017	.222	.033	.284
		IJM	1.012	3.575	.464	1.990
		Univariate	.975	3.837	1.044	.570
	Equal	MMDMD	.020	.222	.036	.342
		IJM	1.102	3.308	.575	1.511
		Univariate	1.082	3.360	.934	1.911
	Higher	MMDMD	.024	.232	.039	.301
		IJM	1.240	2.751	.686	.497
		Univariate	1.326	2.407	1.009	4.484
	Much higher	MMDMD	.028	.259	.044	.218
		IJM	1.463	2.202	.825	.293
		Univariate	1.825	1.570	1.324	5.461

Product Usage	Lower	MMDMD	.013	.196	.038	.329
		IJM	.688	2.094	.286	2.123
		Univariate	.658	2.470	.773	.735
	Equal	MMDMD	.016	.200	.042	.517
		IJM	.730	1.953	.355	.906
		Univariate	.703	2.202	.632	.932
	Higher	MMDMD	.019	.222	.046	.397
		IJM	.785	1.693	.436	.442
		Univariate	.825	1.685	.680	3.321
	Much higher	MMDMD	.022	.251	.050	.094
		IJM	.867	1.495	.544	.089
		Univariate	1.115	1.254	.936	.314

and any shape of the response function. If desired, the response functions for television and magazines may be different.

The exposure estimation component of MMDMD is very accurate, resulting in an average cell error for the 600 random schedules of only .008 and comparable accuracy for the segment-targeted schedules. The exposure estimation component of MMDMD is substantially more accurate than that of the (univariate) model, which treats exposures in different media as being comparable, and that of the model (independent joint model), which considers the media separately. MMDMD's performance is also more robust over a wide range of response assumptions.

Our findings clearly indicate the need for an intergration of the media-planning function. Only through integrated, centralized media planning can the intermedia duplications between the television and magazine subschedules be modeled adequately.

The results lead us to question the common practice of estimating a univariate exposure distribution across media. The univariate model clearly had the worst performance of all models we tested. We provide a model for improving the efficiency of the media-planning process by estimating the joint exposure distribution in a fashion consistent with the complexities inherent in mixed media advertising schedules.

Notes

1. Though this assumption is useful in reducing computation, it introduces error to the extent that vehicles within medium have differences. Even so, these errors tend to be largely eliminated during the aggregation process, as may be seen from past empirical results for the BBD. Journal space limitations preclude a more extended discussion here, but such a discussion is available from the authors.

2. Multinomial expansion requires that the trials be independent. Strictly speaking this should not be the case in the media exposure application, because independence leads to some unwanted theoretical inconsistencies. However, this approximation is necessary to make possible the utilization of the DMD.

3. Conceptually the mechanism underlying the model is n trials from a sample space similar to that shown in figure 4A–1, with an assumption of vehicle homogeneity within medium. The many combinations of events that are possible are embodied by the multinomial distribution.

4. The Leckenby–Kishi DMDH model estimates between-vehicle duplication using the Hofmans-geometric distribution (Leckenby and Kishi 1982a). The probabilities from the estimation are analogues to the probabilities in figure 4A–1, although in the former model the number of exclusive probabilities may be much greater than four, depending on the number of vehicles.

5. Relative effectiveness, as used here, is just one of several response characteristics that are allowed to vary. The usual assumptions of linearity are not made.

6. For example, the response $R(XTOT)$ for $XTOT = 1$ corrsponds to two cells in the joint frequency distribution—$XTV = a$ and $XMAG = 0$, or $XTV = 0$ and $XMAG = 1$. Suppose the first possibility occurs empirically with twice the frequency of the second possibility. Then the "empirically correct" value of $R(1)$ would be two-thirds of the actual response for $XTV = 1$ and $XMAG = 0$, plus one-third of the actual response for $XTV = 0$ and $XMAG = 1$.

References

Aaker, David A. (1975), "ADMOD: An Advertising Decision Model," *Journal of Marketing Research* 12 (February):37–45.

——— and Philip K. Brown (1972), "Evaluating Vehicle Source Effects," *Journal of Advertising Research* 12 (August):11–16.

Advertising Age (1982), "Advertising's Hot One Hundred."

Balachandra, Ramaiya (1975), "Media Selection and Advertising Scheduling Strategy," unpublished Ph.D. dissertation. Columbia University, New York.

Barksdale, Hiram C., Jr. and Jay E. Klompmaker (1979), "Marketing Implications of the Split-Brain Phenomenon." *Proceedings of the Southern Marketing Association,* 284–87.

Bass, Frank M. and Roland T. Lonsdale (1966)," An Exploration of Linear Programming in Media Selection," *Journal of Marketing Research* 3 (May):179–88.

Bogart, Leo, S.B. Tolley, and F. Orenstein (1980), "What One Little Ad Can Do," *Journal of Advertising Research* 10 (August):3–15.

Buchanan, Dodds I. (1964), "How Interest in the Product Affects Recall: Print Ads vs. Commercials," *Journal of Advertising Research* 4 (March):9–14.

Chandon, Jean–Louis Jose (1976), "A Comparative Study of Media Exposure Models," unpublished Ph.D. dissertation, Northwestern University, Evanston, Ill.

Deming, W. Edwards and Frederick F. Stephan (1940), "On a Least Squares Adjustment of a Sampled Frequency Table When the Expected Marginal Totals Are Known," *Annals of Mathematical Statistics* 11:427–44.

Feller, W. (1969), *An Introduction to Probability Theory and Its Applications 1*. New York: John Wiley & Sons.

Gensch, Dennis H. (1969), "A Computer Simulation Model for Selecting Advertising Schedules," *Journal of Marketing Research* 6 (May):203–14.

——— (1970), "Media Factors: A Review Article," *Journal of Marketing Research* 7 (May):216–25.

Goodhardt, G.J. and A.S.C. Ehrenberg (1969), "The Duplication of Viewing between and within Channels." *Journal of Marketing Research* 6 (May):169–78.

Grass, Robert C., and Wallace H. Wallace (1974), "Advertising Communication: Print vs. TV," *Journal of Advertising Research* 14 (October):19–23.

Greene, Jerome D. and J.S. Stock (1967), *Advertising Reach and Frequency in Magazines.* New York: Marketmath and Reader's Digest Association.

Hansen, Flemming (1981), "Hemispheric Lateralization: Implications for Understanding Consumer Behavior," *Journal of Consumer Research* 8 (June):23–36.

Headen, Robert S., Jay Klompmaker, and Roland T. Rust (1979), "The Duplication of Viewing Law and Television Media Schedule Evaluation," *Journal of Marketing Research* 16 (August):333–40.

———, ———, and Jesse E. Teel (1977), "Predicting Audience Exposure to Spot TV Advertising Schedules," *Journal of Marketing Research* 14 (February):1–9.

Hirschman, Elizabeth O. and Michael K. Mills (1980), "Sources Shoppers Use to Pick Stores," *Journal of Advertising Research* 20 (February):47–51.

Hofmans, Pierre (1966), "Measuring the Net Cumulative Coverage of Any Combination of Media," *Journal of Marketing Research* 3:269–78.

Hugues, Michel (1975), "An Empirical Study of Media Comparison," *Journal of Marketing Research* 12 (May):221–23.

Jain, Chaman L. (1975), "Broadcast Support to Newspaper Ads," *Journal of Advertising Research* 15 (October):69–72.

Jeuland, Abel, Frank M. Bass, and Gordon P. Wright (1980), "A Multibrand Stochastic Model Compounding Heterogeneous Erland Timing and Multinomial Choice Processes," *Operations Research* 28 (March–April):255–77.

Johnson, N.L. and S. Kotz (1969), *Discrete Distributions.* Boston: Houghton Mifflin.

——— and ——— (1972), *Continuous Multivariate Distributions.* John Wiley & Sons.

Kalwani, Manohar U. (1980), "Maximum Likelihood Estimation of Zero-Order Models Given Variable Numbers of Purchases per Household," *Journal of Marketing Research* 17 (November):547–51.

Krugman, Herbert E. (1966–67), "The Measurement of Advertising Involvement," *Public Opinion Quarterly* (Winter):583–96.

——— (1971), "Brain Wave Measures of Media Involvement," *Journal of Advertising Research* 11 (February):3–9.

——— (1972), "Why Three Exposures May Be Enough," *Journal of Advertising Research* (December):11–14.

——— (1977), "Memory without Recall, Exposure without Recognition," *Journal of Advertising Research* 17:7–12.

——— (1980a), Letter to the Editor, *Journal of Advertising Research* 20 (June):63.

——— (1980b), "Point of View: Sustained Viewing of Television," *Journal of Advertising Research* 20 (June):65–68.

Kwerel, Seymour M. (1968), "Information Retrieval for Media Planning," *Management Science* 15 (December):B137–60.

Larkin, Ernest F. (1972), "Consumer Perceptions of the Media and Their Advertising Content," *Journal of Advertising* 8 (November):5–48.

Leckenby, John D. and Shizue Kishi (1982a), "Performance of Four Exposure Distribution Models," *Journal of Advertising Research* 22 (April/May):35–44.

——— and ——— (1982b), "The Dirichlet Multinomial Distribution as a Media Exposure Model," unpublished working paper, University of Illinois.

Little, John D.C. and Leonard M. Lodish (1969), "A Media Planning Calculus," *Operations Research* 17 (January–February):1–35.

Lodish, Leonard M. (1973), "Exposure Interactions among Media Schedules," *Journal of Advertising Research* 13 (April):19–22.

McConnell, J. Douglas (1970), "Do Media Vary in Effectiveness?" *Journal of Advertising Research* 10 (October):19–22.

Metheringham, Richard A. (1964), "Measuring the Net Cumulative Coverage of a Print Campaign," *Journal of Advertising Research* 4 (December):23–28.

Prasad, V. Kanti and L. Winston Ring (1976), "Measuring Sales Effects of Some Marketing Mix Variables and Their Interactions," *Journal of Marketing Research* 13 (November):391–96.

Rossiter, John R. (1980), "Point of View: Brain Hemisphere Activity," *Journal of Advertising Research* 20 (October):75–76.

Rust, Roland T. (1979). "A Model for the Selection of Television Advertising Schedules," unpublished Ph.D. dissertation, University of North Carolina.

——— and Jay E. Klompmaker (1981), "Improving the Estimation Procedure for the Beta Binomial TV Exposure Model," *Journal of Marketing Research* 18 (November):442–48.

———, ———, and Robert S. Headen (1981), "A Comparative Study of Television Duplication Models," *Journal of Advertising* 10:42–46.

Sabavala, Darius J. and Donald G. Morrison (1977), "Television Show Loyalty: A Beta Binomial Model Using Recall Data," *Journal of Advertising Research* 17: 35–43.

——— and ——— (1981), "A Nonstationary Model of Binary Choice Applied to Media Exposure," *Management Science* 27 (June):637–57.

Schreiber, Robert J. (1974), "Instability in Media Exposure Habits," *Journal of Advertising Research* 14:13–17.

Sexton, Donald E., Jr. (1970), "Estimating Marketing Policy Effects on Sales of a Frequently Purchased Product," *Journal of Marketing Research* 6 (August): 338–47.

Shoemaker, Robert W., Richard Staelin, Joseph B. Kadane, and F. Robert Shoaf (1977), "Relation of Brand Choice to Purchase Frequency," *Journal of Marketing Research* 14 (November):458–68.

Simmons Media Studies (1978a), *Selective Markets and the Media Reaching Them.* New York: Simmons Media Studies.

——— (1978b). *Technical Guide: 1977/1978 Study of Selective Markets and the Media Reaching Them.* New York: Simmons Media Studies.

Simon, Julian L. and Johan Arndt (1980), "The Shape of the Advertising Response Function," *Journal of Advertising Research* 20 (August):11–28.

Sperry, Roger W. (1973), "Lateral Specialization of Cerebral Function in the Surgically Separated Hemispheres" in *The Psychology of Thinking,* F.J. McGuigan and R.A. Schoonerer, eds. New York: Academic Press, 209–29.

Srinivasan, V. (1976), "Decomposition of a Multi-Period Media Scheduling Model in Terms of Single Period Equivalents," *Management Science* 23:349–60.

Weinstein, Sidney, Valentine Appel, and Curt Weinstein (1980), "Brain-Activity Responses to Magazine and Television Advertising," *Journal of Advertising Research* 20 (June):57–63.

Zufryden, Fred S. (1973), "Media Scheduling: A Stochastic Dynamic Model Approach," *Management Science* 19:1395–1406.

5
Media Selection Models

Media selection models attempt to select optimal media schedules, given a budget constraint (usually) and facts about the vehicles under consideration. They are thus much more ambitious than any of the models considered so far in the book. Media selection models have undergone an extensive evolution in the past twenty-five years, and significant advances are still being made.

Algorithms for media selection may be classified into three main types: mathematical programming, simulation, and heuristics. Currently the advances are being made not in improvement of the algorithms, but in improving the interface with the user. Some modelers seek to construct user-friendly decision support systems—self-contained, easy-to-use computer systems which include a data base and computer programs for schedule evaluation and selection. The ADSTAR system is an example.

Another means of improving the interface with the user is the expert system approach, which seeks to mimic the reactions of an experienced media planner. Andy Mitchell of the University of Toronto is currently developing such a system.

Mathematical Programming Models

In the early 1960s, mathematical programming formulations of the media selection problem gained great popularity. A mathematical program (not to be confused with a computer program) seeks to find an optimal level for decision variables, such that an "objective function" (which might be equal to profit, reach, or sales, for example) is given the best possible value. There are "constraints" which limit the values the variables may assume. For example a constraint usually seen in media selection models is that the costs of the vehicles must sum to not more than the budget.

There are many varieties of mathematical programming, including linear programming, dynamic programming, goal programming, and integer programming. All are conceptually similar. An explanation of the differences between the different programming techniques is beyond the scope of this book, but a good reference is Wagner.[27]

Maffei developed a dynamic programming model to solve a very small media selection problem as early as 1960.[21] This model served only to illustrate the possibility of applying mathematical programming methods to the media selection problem, since the model had many limitations. In particular, only three vehicles were considered, and each was assumed to serve a different market (a very unrealistic assumption). Other linear programming pioneers were Miller and Starr, who proposed one of the earliest models for media selection.[22]

The first widely heralded model was the BBDO linear programming (LP) model, which was introduced in 1961. Trade publications such as *Advertising Age* carried ads claiming impressive cost savings through the use of the model. The 1962 Midwest Conference of the Advertising Research Foundation (ARF) included an almost hard-sell presentation of the model by Wilson and Maneloveg.[28] The media practitioners, many of whom were mathematically unsophisticated, developed high expectations which could not be met by the simple LP model.

Meanwhile, however, the academic journals reflected the industry trend. Day assessed the viability of linear programming media models in 1962.[11] He concluded that "media selection models can aid in the development of sounder media practices," but only if the modeler is wary of the "difficulties and dangers involved in using complex mathematical models." Two years later, Kotler introduced a rough model which rejected the linear programming assumption of linear response to additional ads.[17] Although he proposed a nonlinear response function, he was unable to complete the computational details necessary to operationalize the model. Stasch introduced a satisficing model (one which aspired to an adequate level rather than an optimal level) which minimized cost.[26] In it he expanded the LP model to incorporate time period and geographical area considerations.

Almost immediately, advertising professionals became disillusioned with linear programming models. Many in the profession generalized their disenchantment to include all computer media models. Canter exemplified this new bias against computers in his 1963 Advertising Research Foundation (ARF) address.[9] He stated that media modelers were "using computers to provide prolific results from inadequate data which can only lead to conclusions of uncertain validity and utility." He went so far as to suggest "a moratorium on computer use in media selection." This disillusionment of over twenty years ago still to some extent poisons industry acceptance of advanced analytical methods.

Although an attitude of skepticism toward media models had been established, work continued both in industry and academia. Broadbent presented a limited overview of a refined LP model in the 1965 ARF conference.[5] His presentation was particularly interesting in that it revealed the use of the media model to determine sensitivities to the input data. In other words, how much difference would it make if there were a particular amount of error in the ratings data, or if the response to advertising were estimated incorrectly. Broadbent concluded that the choice of media schedule was insensitive to the magnitude and shape of the response function, and was insensitive to the ratings of the vehicles used. This last insensitivity was deemed especially important, due to widespread mistrust of published ratings.

Brown and Warshaw introduced a somewhat more complicated method for using linear programming.[8] They made the first operational attempt to relax the assumptions of linearity which were impeding acceptance of the linear programming models. In particular they relaxed the dubious assumption of the linearity of the objective function. The most obvious method for solving a media selection problem involving a nonlinear objective function is to determine the Lagrangian[27] and solve using the Kuhn–Tucker conditions.[18] Unfortunately this procedure leads to overwhelming computational complexities. For that reason they used an alternative means of treating the nonlinear objective function. They approximated the objective function by a series of line segments. Thus decomposed, the objective function could be evaluated on each segment, and then summed.

While this development improved the linear programming method, most of the problems of the LP were still present. In particular the issue of duplication between vehicles was not considered. None of the linear programming models considered the problem of audience accumulation and frequency distributions of exposure.

Integer programming was proposed as a media selection tool by Zangwill.[29] The formulation was essentially that of the linear programming models, with the inclusion of objective function terms for duplication and estimated triplication between vehicles in the schedule. The method is extremely cumbersome computationally, which led Zangwill to suggest that only a small number of schedules be considered. These might be supplied in an initial stage by linear programming.

Bass and Lonsdale produced a linear programming model in 1966.[3] This model was essentially the same as earlier models, but used a different construct as its objective function. A vehicle's weighted exposure units, defined as the rating adjusted for vehicle appropriateness and demographics, were the criteria for optimization. The Bass and Lonsdale model, as the authors freely admitted, was still prey to the crucial linearity problems endemic to linear programming models. In addition their scheme of weighting demographics permitted "double counting" within the target audience, in that an eighteen-year-old male, for example, might be counted in both the 18–21 age segment and the male sex segment.

Introduced by Little and Lodish in 1966, the original MEDIAC is a dynamic programming model.[19] Besides incorporating a time dimension, the model employs a very realistic set of constraints, including consideration of conditional probability of exposure and seasonality.

Unfortunately the model has several serious defects. Most seriously, the model is unable to consider a large number of possible schedules, due to computational complexity. Little and Lodish use a construct they call "exposure efficiency," which is expected number of exposures per capita to a particular vehicle within a particular segment. Thus average frequency is addressed, without concern for reach or the frequency distribution of exposure. Thus much of the information considered important by media planners is ignored in the original MEDIAC. Because of these problems, in 1969, Little and Lodish revised their model to a heuristic formulation which is described later in the chapter.

Goal programming was proposed for the media selection problem by Charnes, Cooper, DeVoe, Learner, and Reinecke.[10] Their goal program, which they called LP II, was the replacement for the original linear programming model they had developed for BBDO. Its method of estimating frequency distributions of exposure uses the lognormal distribution, which is introduced without theoretical justification or empirical defense.

Goal programming forces the media schedule to meet, but not exceed, predetermined goals. Thus it is not an optimization model, and maximum impact is not claimed. Through clever manipulations of the weights in the model, however, one may allow the model to exceed its expectations.

More recently, deKluyver[12] has exhumed the goal programming technique, using the innovation of hard and soft constraints.[16] In the deKluyver method, hard constraints (constraints that must be met) have top priority in the goal programming costing hierarchy, while soft constraints (constraints that are desired but not necessary) have second priority. While deKluyver's formulation is an interesting advance, most of the problems of linear programming still remain.

In summary, use of mathematical programming techniques of media schedule selection was a promising approach which never performed acceptably at a practical level due to two major failings, both in large part stemming from the crippling requirement of linearity. First, the ability of the method to incorporate realistic constraints is severely limited. Second, the method cannot naturally account for duplication, and thus poorly estimates frequency distributions of exposure. These difficulties encouraged the development of simulation and heuristic techniques, which are discussed next.

Simulation Models

The widespread utilization of computers made the simulation technique popular in many fields during the late 1960s. In the selection of media schedules, simulation has two strong advantages over mathematical programming techniques. First, it is able to explicitly take into account the frequency distribution of exposure, since each simulated individual is exposed a particular number of times. The full frequency distribution provides the media planner with more information than the usual summary statistics such as GRPs, reach, and average frequency. Also, and particularly important, this frequency may be combined with a response function to give the value of the schedule.

Second, a much greater degree of realism may be incorporated, since imposed mathematical forms and distributions are seldom used. Thus simulation was very attractive to media modelers of the late 1960s. Unfortunately simulation had one serious flaw: the staggering amount of computer time required to simulate even a small media selection problem. Thus simulation is typically used to evaluate particular schedules rather than to select among possible schedules. Usually a handful of possible schedules is chosen judgmentally or by other means. The simulation then estimates the frequency distribution of exposure for each schedule. Each frequency distribution is then combined with a response function. The schedule with the highest value is then judged most promising.

An early simulation model was the CAM (computer assessment of media) model, used by the London Press Exchange and presented by Broadbent at the ARF conference.[6] This model transforms actual viewing or readership data into probabilities of exposure for particular individuals. Random numbers are then generated, which determine whether or not each hypothetical individual was, in "fact," exposed to a particular vehicle. Another early simulation model was the Simulmatics model.[4]

The most important simulation model is Gensch's AD–ME–SIM.[14] The model uses several kinds of media weights. "Target population weights" permit the emphasis of particular demographic groups. For example, a beer company would place higher weights on the male sex and the 18–35 age group. "Vehicle appropriateness weights" allow for the nonrating factors that influence the effectiveness of an ad. For example, a greeting card company might find that a television drama put viewers into the right mood to be receptive to their product. "Commercial exposure weights" involve the conditional probability of being exposed to a commercial within a vehicle, given that one has been exposed to the vehicle. If people leave the room often during a television program, for example, that program will have a low commercial exposure weight. "Commercial perception weights" deal with levels of conscious perception of the ad. The idea here is that the ad is more effective when people pay attention to it.

Friedman proposed a simulation model which uses mutually exclusive market segments, which are treated as homogeneous.[13] This method is computationally simpler and more limited than Gensch's, but is otherwise not an improvement.

In conclusion, simulation models of media schedule selection, like mathematical programming models, were fatally deficient, although promising. They were good at incorporating realistic constraints and estimating frequency distribution of exposure. They were intolerably poor in their ability to scan a large number of schedules.

A method was needed that was more realistic than mathematical programming, but computationally more feasible than simulation. The compromise candidate, heuristic assessment, is discussed next.

Heuristic Models

A heuristic is a set procedure for obtaining a good solution which is not necessarily optimal. Heuristics have never been as glamorous as mathematical optimization techniques or simulation models. They are used simply because they work better in many instances. In the media schedule selection problem, heuristics have been around since the early 1960s. Since then, however, heuristic media models have advanced impressively in sophistication.

Young and Rubicam's HIGH ASSAY model, sketched by Moran at the 1962 ARF conference, is an early heuristic model.[23] Its logic is based on adding vehicles to a schedule based on marginal contribution (in cost per thousand, adjusted by source effects, copy effectiveness, and other factors) to the schedule. Although naive by today's standards, the HIGH ASSAY model was an improvement over the simplistic linear programming models which were then in vogue.

Brown proposed a variation on the marginal analysis theme.[7] His model was widely criticized for both technical and practical reasons.[25 and 2] The most damaging criticism, leveled by both Schreiber and Banks, was that Brown's method of assigning probability of exposure was faulty.

According to Brown, in an error replicated by many others, if a respondent "claims to have read four of the last six issues . . . his probability . . . is taken to be 4/6." This method of probability assignment is known as "actuarial assignment," and has often been criticized. If these actuarial probabilities are used to attempt to reproduce the original data, they fail miserably. There is a strong bias away from the middle frequency classes, while the outer frequency classes are inflated.

Nevertheless, as Schreiber and Banks point out, the binomial theorem may be used to determine expected frequency class sizes, for a given distribution of probabilities. If the problem above is viewed as a probabilistic outcome of six trials, the probabilities assigned should be different. This conceptual approach is used in the better accepted "personal probability" method.[15]

The three most advanced among the published heuristic models are discussed next.

MEDIAC

Little and Lodish updated their mathematical programming model, MEDIAC, using a heuristic approach. The new MEDIAC, introduced in 1969, incorporated many advanced features.[20] Because the article describing the new MEDIAC is quite technical, much detail is avoided in the discussion in this chapter. The original article is reprinted at the end of this chapter.

Perhaps the most advanced feature of MEDIAC was its on-line nature. It was interactive, permitting its direct use at a computer teletype. MEDIAC foreshadowed the PC interactive systems to be developed fifteen years later.

Central to the MEDIAC model is the assumption of dynamic exposure effects. This means that the time component is explicitly taken into account, and individuals forget ads over time. This is a realistic assumption which greatly complicates the model. Complicating the model in this particular way means that in order to maintain tractability, other parts of the model need to be made more simple. We shall see that the exposure estimation component of the model is what suffers the most.

Individuals are assumed to have an "exposure level" which is related to response. The exposure level increases when an individual is exposed to an ad, and otherwise decreases over time, due to forgetting.

These aspects are mathematically straightforward. The problems with MEDIAC arise from the estimation of the distribution of the exposure level. The mathematics of exposure in MEDIAC are fairly advanced and will not be considered in detail here, but they depend upon estimating duplication, as is shown in chapter 3. As demonstrated in that chapter, the pairwise duplication estimation procedure proposed by Little and Lodish does not perform very well. Even so, MEDIAC relies upon the duplication estimates even more.

If y is the exposure level of an individual, r_i is the probability that the individual will be exposed to vehicle i, and r_{ij} is the estimated probability of exposure to vehicles i and j (identical to duplication within a segment), then the moments of y are

$$E[y] = \sum r_i \tag{5.1}$$

$$E[y^2] = \sum r_i + 2\sum\sum r_{ij} \tag{5.2}$$

The higher moments are also required for the exposure estimation procedure, and they are not functions solely of the ratings and duplications. Thus Little and Lodish recommend plotting the higher moments as a function of the lower ones. This is a very ad hoc procedure, and is especially troublesome considering that the duplications are likely to be (bad) estimates in the first place. Exact equations for estimating the higher moments are not given, and the authors admit their inability to develop appropriate equations.

ADMOD

Aaker[1] introduced ADMOD as a successor to MEDIAC. In spite of his protests to the contrary, it is essentially similar to MEDIAC. To the best of my knowledge ADMOD has never been fully operationalized.

ADMOD evaluates response in terms of particular cognitive changes which are specified by a media plan. This appears at first glance to be a revolutionary change, but actually MEDIAC is capable of doing that with no change in the overall mathematical framework. Only the response function would change. Thus this distinction does not really make much difference from a modeling standpoint.

The major difference from MEDIAC is in the way exposure is handled. ADMOD is not a dynamic model, as is MEDIAC, and thus is capable of complicating the exposure estimation component of the model. Aaker suggests taking a sample from each relevant market segment. Each individual in the sample is then assigned a probability of exposure to each vehicle, based on historical data. The inferior actuarial assignment method seems implied, although precise details are not given.

The individual probabilities are then used to estimate the exposure distribution, using simulation. Aaker claims that ADMOD "considers exposure probabilities at the level of individuals without resorting to simulation,"[1] but that is clearly not the case if individual exposure probabilities are used.

Aaker concedes that the above method quickly results in prohibitive computational requirements. Therefore he recommends the use of the binomial distribution. His revised binomial distribution, as reviewed in chapter 4, performs much worse than other exposure estimation methods. Thus, like MEDIAC, ADMOD suffers from reliance upon a poor exposure estimation component.

It is clear that the direction for improvement of heuristic media selection models was the incorporation of improved methods of exposure estimation. The ADSTAR system, discussed next, includes a heuristic selection method which includes advanced exposure estimation components.

ADSTAR: A Decision Support System for Media Selection

The ADSTAR system is a PC-based decision support system for media selection. It is entirely menu-driven, which makes it unusually user-friendly. The user simply responds to cues on a video screen. No programming knowledge is required. There is virtually no start-up time for learning the system. A beginner is prompted at every step by the terminal.

ADSTAR's selection methods are a refinement of VIDEAC,[24] a model for selecting network television advertising schedules. The model is similar in many respects to its predecessors, MEDIAC, AD–ME–SIM, and ADMOD, with the notable exception of its much more sophisticated exposure estimation methods. Because exposure estimation is of pivotal importance in a media selection model, a substantial improvement in that area inevitably results in a substantially better model.

The exposure methods used involve for each medium the best methods discovered by the empirical research reported in chapters 3 and 4. The beta binomial distribution is employed, using estimated duplications. For intermedia exposure, the Dirichlet multinomial distribution is used.

The ADSTAR system is fully self-contained, including data files, model programs, and communication programs. It is scheduled to be operational on the IBM PC and PC-XT by summer 1986.

The system has many capabilities. The user may enter data concerning ratings, duplications (if available), target markets, budget, and many other details. As a rule, only essential inputs, such as ratings, are absolutely required, with other potential inputs automatically set at default values. These default values may be overriden by the user if he or she so desires.

Once the data are entered, reports may be easily obtained summarizing the data. This function is facilitated by the fact that the system is written to employ the features of the RBASE 5000 data base package.

ADSTAR is primarily designed for the selection and evaluation of prospective media schedules. The media selection mode enables the interactive selection of a media schedule, targeted to any segment or segments.

Evaluation of hypothetical schedules is also accomplished by ADSTAR. Thus the system estimates response to a suggested schedule, as well as suggests improvements to the schedule. This feature is especially useful in negotiation, because the system supplies information quickly about the value of a schedule and how it might be improved.

Conclusion

Media selection models have evolved considerably in the past twenty-five years. The most advanced of the current models (as typified by ADSTAR) now employ advanced exposure estimation methods, efficient heuristic search routines, and, most importantly, an easy-to-use PC-based decision support system with advanced data base capabilities.

References

1. David A. Aaker, "ADMOD: An Advertising Decision Model," *Journal of Marketing Research* (February 1975):37–45.

2. Seymour Banks, "The True Probability of Exposure," *Journal of Marketing Research* (May 1968):223–24.

3. Frank M. Bass and Ronald T. Lonsdale, "An Exploration of Linear Programming in Media Selection," *Journal of Marketing Research* (May 1966):179–88.

4. Alex Bernstein, "Computer Simulation of Media Exposure" in *A Report of the 6th Meeting of the ARF Operations Research Discussion Group* (New York: Advertising Research Foundation, 1961).

5. Simon R. Broadbent, "A Year's Experience of the LPE Media Model," in *ARF 11th Annual Conference Proceedings* (New York: Advertising Research Foundation, October 1965):51–56.

6. Simon R. Broadbent, "Media Planning and Computers by 1970: A Review of the Use of Mathematical Models in Media Planning," *Applied Statistics* (November 1966):240–41.

7. Douglas B. Brown, "A Practical Procedure for Media Selection," *Journal of Marketing Research* (August 1967):262–69.

8. Douglas B. Brown and Martin R. Warshaw, "Media Selection by Linear Programming," *Journal of Marketing Research* (February 1965):83–88.

9. Stanley F. Canter, "Have Computers Lived up to Their Promises for Media Selection?" in *ARF 9th Annual Conference Proceedings* (New York: Advertising Research Foundation, October 1963):84–88.

10. A. Charnes, W.W. Cooper, J.K. DeVoe, D.B. Learner, and W. Reinecke, "A Goal Programming Model for Media Planning," *Management Science* (April 1968):423–30.

11. Ralph L. Day, "Linear Programming in Media Selection," *Journal of Advertising Research* (June 1962):40–44.

12. Cornelius A. deKluyver, "Hard and Soft Constraints in Media Scheduling," *Journal of Advertising Research* (June 1978):27–31.

13. Lawrence Friedman, "Constructing a Media Simulation Model," *Journal of Advertising Research* (August 1970):33–39.

14. Dennis H. Gensch, "A Computer Simulation Model for Selecting Advertising Schedules," *Journal of Marketing Research* (May 1969):203–14.

15. Jerome D. Greene, "Personal Media Probabilities," *Journal of Advertising Research* (October 1970):12–18.

16. J.W. Kendall, "Hard and Soft Constraints in Linear Programming," *OMEGA* (1975):709–15.

17. Phillip Kotler, "Toward an Explicit Model for Media Selection," *Journal of Advertising Research* (March 1964):34–41.

18. H.W. Kuhn and A.W. Tucker, "Linear Inequalities and Related Systems" in *Annals of Mathematical Studies* (Princeton, N.J.: Princeton University Press, 1956).

19. John D.C. Little and Leonard M. Lodish, "A Media Selection Model and Its Optimization by Dynamic Programming," *Industrial Management Review* (Fall 1966):15–24.

20. John D.C. Little and Leonard M. Lodish, "A Media Planning Calculus," *Operations Research* (January–February 1969):1–35.

21. Richard B. Maffei, "Planning Advertising Expenditures by Dynamic Programming Methods," *Management Technology* (December 1960):94–100.

22. D.W. Miller and M.K. Starr, *Executive Decisions and Operations Research* (Englewood Cliffs, N.J.: Prentice–Hall, 1960).

23. William T. Moran, "Practical Media Models–What Must They Look Like?" in *ARF 8th Annual Conference Proceedings* (New York: Advertising Research Foundation, October 1962), pp. 30–38.

24. Roland T. Rust, "Selecting Network Television Advertising Schedules," *Journal of Business Research,* forthcoming.

25. Robert J. Schreiber, "A Practical Procedure for Media Selection: Comments," *Journal of Marketing Research* (May 1968):221–22.

26. Stanley F. Stasch, "Linear Programming and Space–Time Considerations in Media Selection," *Journal of Advertising Research* (December 1965):40–46.

27. Harvey M. Wagner, *Principles of Operations Research,* 2nd edition (Englewood Cliffs, N.J.: Prentice–Hall, 1975).

28. Clark L. Wilson and Herbert Maneloveg, "A Year of LP Media Planning for Clients" in *ARF Midwest Conference* (New York: Advertising Research Foundation, November 1962), pp. 78–89.

29. Willard I. Zangwill, "Media Selection by Decision Programming," *Journal of Advertising Research* (September 1965):30–36.

Appendix 5A: A Media Planning Calculus

John D.C. Little
Leonard M. Lodish

An advertiser buys space and time in advertising media to tell prospective customers about his product. He normally hopes that the information in his advertisements will lead people to buy his product and that they will become satisfied customers. He presumably intends the extra sales generated to yield a net profit.

The role of media in advertising, therefore, is to convey messages to prospects. Media are chosen in the course of constructing an advertising plan, the steps of which include: (1) setting the budget, (2) identifying the audience, (3) picking the advertising message, (4) preparing the copy treatment, and (5) selecting the media. The steps are not independent. Message, copy, and media all depend on the audience to be reached. Budget sets the scale of the whole operation. However, once budget and audience characteristics are set, the questions of message and copy can be fairly well separated from the question of how to expose the audience to the messages efficiently. Only the media question will be taken up here, although the other planning steps affect our formulation, because provision must be made for give and take between media selection and the rest of the plan.

The media planning problem may be stated as follows: Given a set of media options, a budget, and various data about the media and the audience to be reached, which options should be used and when should they be used in order to maximize profit or some related measure of performance? By a media option we ordinarily mean a detailed specification of the place, position, size, and other outward characteristics of an advertisement, but not

---

 The work reported herein was supported (in part) by Project MAC, an MIT research program sponsored by the Advanced Research Projects Agency, U.S. Department of Defense, under an Office of Naval Research contract.

The authors wish to thank Fred Anderson for his help in developing the material on the higher moments shown in figure 5A–3 and Charles Meyer and Fred Nagel for their help in developing duplication formulas and the data shown in figure 5A–4.

the message and copy treatment. Why is the media problem challenging? Because of the multiplicity of seemingly reasonable choices usually available, because of the complexity of advertising phenomena, and because of the quantity of media decisions that must be made.

Our goal is to build a media model that will increase advertising productivity. This requires that the model lead people to make better media decisions; it requires the model to be economical to use; and it requires that the model be, in fact, used.

To establish that the model will increase productivity is difficult. Certain of the required inputs will be subjective. Many aspects of the advertising effectiveness process are poorly understood. The most satisfactory test of validity would be to predict outcomes (for example, sales) and compare them with actual results, but the inherent variability in sales and the problem of relating sales to advertising when other marketing variables also affect response make this difficult.

Considering these obstacles, perhaps we should give up, at least until the underlying processes are better understood. Media planners obviously do not have this option. They must do something sensible with the information they have. Furthermore, they have to do this in the midst of day-to-day pressures. The important questions then are: Can we isolate the most relevant phenomena for media planning, can we put them together into a consistent structure, and can we link the media planner to the structure in a practical way? We claim the answers are yes.

Our final product will be called a media planning calculus. By a "calculus" we mean a system of numerical procedures for transforming data and judgments into a schedule. The model supplies the structure, the user supplies the data and judgments, and the computer supplies the muscle.

What then are some of the facts and phenomena essential to media selection? The main purpose of media is to deliver messages to potential customers efficiently. Relevant to this are at least the following ideas:

1. *Market segments* for classifying customers,
2. *Sales potentials* for each segment,
3. *Exposure probabilities* for each media option in each segment,
4. *Media costs.*

Advertisers spread their campaigns over time. Why? One reason is that the effect of advertising tends to wear off. This is demonstrable; Vidale and Wolfe,[1] for example, display data showing the effect. Another reason is that advertising is often considered most valuable near the time of purchase, and people enter and leave the market continuously. Implicit in both these reasons is the idea that people tend to forget past exposures. In addition, both sales potential and media-exposure probability may vary with time of year. Therefore, we add the following phenomena:

5. *Forgetting* by people exposed to advertising,
6. *Seasonality* in product potential and media audience.

A recurring concern in making advertising decisions is the effect of diminishing returns. A person has only so much ability to buy a product. After some point, further advertising to him will be wasted. The phenomenon has been amply observed in practice; see, for example, Benjamin and Maitland.[2] The diminishing returns effect is one part of the more general phenomenon of customer response. We conclude that any media selection model should consider:

7. *Individual response* to exposure, including the effect of diminishing returns.

Media planners and media data services frequently pay considerable attention to audience duplication; see, for example, Metheringham.[3] Discussions often centers around reach and frequency. The *reach of a media schedule* is usually defined as the fraction of people who are in the audience of at least one vehicle of the schedule. *Frequency* is defined as the average number of times a person is in the audience of a schedule, given that he is in the audience at least once. In terms of advertising objectives, however, more important than a person being in the audience is his actual exposure to the advertising message. We wish to consider the more basic information of how many people receive zero exposures, one exposure, two exposures, etc., and further how these are spread over time. This information is needed to assess the expected response of the various individuals in the audience and so deduce the response of the market as a whole. Therefore, we take into account:

8. The *distribution of exposures* over people and over time.

Finally, provision must be made for putting the exposures from different media options onto a common basis; that is, it must be possible to assign relative values or weights to exposures in each option. This is always done implicitly in designing a media schedule; in a formal model it is done explicitly. We therefore add consideration of:

9. *Exposure value* for the exposures in each media option.

These, then, are minimum specifications of data and phenomena to include in a useful media model. More could be added. However, these are already more than are ordinarily used now. Most media planning is rather macroscopic, with principal attention going (perhaps quite rightly) to audience potential and simple efficiency measures like cost per thousand, sometimes with a side investigation of reach. We want to show how more phenomena can be handled with greater ease than these usually are today.

To be productive, a model must be used. To be used it should be readily available and inexpensive to operate. Modern time-shared computers with remote on-line terminals make this possible. They permit immediate access to the computer, English language communication, user-instructing programs, and low cost per use. In our system, the media planner supplies data for his own problem and he or his staff runs it. He can think about his problem at the terminal, asking questions of the model and making changes in the schedule in a problem-solving dialog.

To summarize, our goal is productivity; our approach is to set up a structure embodying the principal phenomena relevant to media selection and, through time-shared computing, make it easy and inexpensive to use. We cite the following reasons for believing that this approach will be productive. The computer is an enthusiastic clerk. Given a model, it can evaluate many more alternatives within reasonable time and cost limits than can people. A computer can handle complexity with ease, for example, local media mixed with national media across several market segments. Changes are easy to make; therefore, there can be give and take between media selection and the rest of the advertising planning process. Sensitivity analyses can easily be made; that is, data and assumptions can be changed to see whether they appreciably affect the outcome. This is advantageous because much advertising data is surrounded by uncertainty and controversy. The model is flexible and permits trying out a variety of assumptions. Perhaps most important, however, a model provides a unified structure for organizing the central issues of the problem. Requirements for data and judgments are defined. Criteria are chosen and consistently applied. This seems certain to bring forth better data, more careful judgments, and more relevant criteria.

The remainder of this analysis is divided into the following major sections: (1) literature review, (2) model, (3) optimization, (4) data considerations, (5) the on-line system, and (6) discussion. For ease of presentation the model section is further subdivided into (1) exposure concepts, (2) market response, (3) exposure arithmetic, (4) budget constraint, (5) end effects, and (6) the mathematical program.

Literature Review

The literature on mathematical models for media selection starts about 1960, although as early as 1946 Banks[35] developed an incremental analysis of media that contained a number of key ideas. In 1960, a simple, hypothetical media problem was formulated as a linear program by Miller and Starr.[4] Soon after came the major pioneering work on linear programming models done jointly by BBDO and CEIR. Descriptions of this may be found in Wilson[5] and Buzzell.[6] The linear programming approach has been further discussed by Day,[7] Engel and Warshaw,[8] Stasch,[9] and Bass and Lonsdale.[10]

In all published examples of these linear programs, the objective function is linear in the number of exposures. This implies that the value of ten exposures to one person is the same as that of one exposure to each of ten people. Such an assumption does not seem reasonable, particularly at high levels of exposure, where additional exposures are ordinarily believed to have less value than previous ones. The effect of linearity on the solution is that the most efficient medium for generating exposures will usually be bought until some upper limit is reached, then the next most efficient will be bought until its limit is reached, and so on. Upper limits must be provided to prevent unreasonable schedules. However, this starts to look similar to picking a schedule without a model, except for the important point that the methods are systematic and explicit.

To get away from strict linearity, diminishing returns and other forms of market response were introduced. Kotler,[11] for example, presents a nonlinear model. In an unpublished paper reporting on the BBDO–CEIR work, Godfrey[12] outlines a method of dealing with certain types of nonlinearities. Wilson[5] refers briefly to a method, and presumably it is the same one. More recently, Brown and Warshaw[13] have published essentially the same thing. The basis of this method is a standard device for converting a nonlinear program into a linear one in the case that the objective function is separable (that is, is the sum of functions, each of a single variable) and, for a maximization problem, concave (that is, the functions are linear or show diminishing returns, but never increasing returns). All three of these nonlinear models have a serious drawback in that the nonlinearities of each medium are separate. Thus, a person's increase in response from seeing an ad in *Life* is the same whether he has seen zero, one, or ten ads in some other magazine. It would seem more reasonable to expect diminishing returns with total exposure.

Several further difficulties beset most of the above formulations. First, the timing of the insertions over the planning period is usually ignored, or at least set outside the model. Exceptions are Godfrey[12] and Stasch[9] who propose to allocate over time by introducing additional variables and additional constraints. Once again, however, the borderline between setting the constraints and setting the schedule tends to blur. The next difficulty is that the treatment of audience duplication is usually weak or nonexistent. Finally, a linear program permits variables to take on fractional values, whereas the number of insertions must always be an integer.

Zangwill[14] suggests handling the integrality problem by using integer programming, but the current state of the art in this field is not encouraging for problems of the size encountered in media selection. Furthermore, as in many of the models, Zangwill's evaluation of the effectiveness of a media choice is done almost entirely outside the model. While this may be said to offer great flexibility, much of the appeal of a model lies in having it synthesize the effectiveness of a schedule out of events that are happening at the consumer level.

Recently, Charnes, Cooper, DeVoe, Learner, and Reinecke[15] have introduced LP II, a successor to Mediametrics. Time is considered, although not forgetting. Audience duplication is brought in under the assumption of independence between media. The objective function is a weighted combination of the magnitudes of differences between target and actual values of a set of goals. The goals might include target frequencies in each market segment and more complex quantities such as "reaching 85 percent of the kth audience segment at time t_1." In the examples shown, the schedule is penalized for exceeding a goal as well as for not reaching it. The choice of goals and their weights is made by the user.

Another major line of attack on media selection is microsimulation (the following of individuals through time in their media actions). An early model of this type was built by the Simulmatics Corporation.[16] The output was patterns of exposure without evaluation or optimization. Moran[17] reports a simulation model but gives little detail. Brown[18] and Gensch[19] do not include time effects but do treat people individually.

The virtue of microsimulation is its potential comprehensiveness. Many phenomena can be put into the model with comparative ease. This is a mixed blessing, since the problems of model construction and testing, data gathering, and computer running time go up rapidly as detail increases. There is a danger that much of the computer time will be spent pursuing issues not really central to the decision at hand. A difficulty inherent in the simulation of individuals is that of attaining sample sizes large enough for adequate evaluation of a schedule, particularly when the schedule contains media vehicles with small audiences. Furthermore, the search for improved schedules tends to become expensive because each separate schedule evaluation may take considerable computing time. Partly for this reason, the search for improvement is frequently left outside the computer.

The discussion so far has centered on work done in the United States. Work done in England goes back in time as far or further, has generally taken different directions and has been of excellent quality. Lee and Burkart,[20] Taylor,[21] Lee,[22,23] and Ellis[24] have developed a series of models motivated especially by print media. Several of the models were stimulated by problems arising at British European Airways and have been applied there. These models are much more explicit in their treatment of exposure probabilities and individual response to exposure than those previously mentioned. Under certain sets of assumptions, easily applied rules for optimal media selection are worked out mathematically. In the more complicated models, which take into account market response over time, the optimization is left as an integer programming problem.

Beale, Hughes, and Broadbent[25] describe the London Press Exchange model for media schedule assessment. This is a major model brought to the point of practical application. The authors call their model a simulation, but it is perhaps fair to say that much of their computational efficiency can be traced to clever circumvention of straight simulation. The model is flexible and computable, and has been built around a considerable base of data. One notable lack is any treatment of the effect of time; there is, for example, no forgetting. The search for schedule improvement is outside the computer, although provision is made for multiple simultaneous schedule evaluations.

There are at least two reported French media models. Steinberg, Comes, and Barache[26] present a model of expected response to advertising exposures. The distribution of exposures is obtained by simulation and assumes independence of exposure opportunities. Bertier and DuJeu[27] develop a careful simulation of the distribution of exposures from a schedule of print media.

We relate the present work to our earlier paper.[28] The model there incorporates nonlinear response, market segmentation, and forgetting, and is optimized by dynamic programming. However, the latter becomes computationally prohibitive with more than one or two market segments. Franzi[29] has investigated separable programming methods for optimizing the model, but the problem of fractional solutions remains, and in this present analysis we have moved away from exact optimization to heuristic methods.

A key technical innovation of the present model is a new method of calculating expected response. Response is expanded as a power series in exposure level. Expected response then becomes a weighted sum of the moments of the exposure-level distribution. It is shown that the first two moments (the most important ones) require only readily available and easily manageable media coverage and duplication data. As a result, the calculation of expected response is very efficient. By comparison, if expected response were obtained by simulating individuals and averaging over them, the calculation might take a hundred or a thousand times as long for the same accuracy. The speed of the basic calculation is used to gain two important advantages. First, it permits a maximum-seeking search over thousands of possible schedules and, second, it makes an on-line system feasible because answers to moderately sized problems can be obtained in a short time.

There exists a variety of commercially secret or otherwise incompletely published work. We are aware of some of it, but obviously cannot adequately review it. We would be glad to have the opportunity.

Model

The model may be described briefly as follows: The population is divided into *market segments.* People in each segment have their own *sales potential* and media habits. A media schedule consists of *insertions* in *media options.* An insertion brings about *exposures* to people in one or more market segments. The exposures serve to increase the *exposure level* of individuals in the segment. However, people are subject to *forgetting,* and so the retained exposure level decays with time in the absence of new exposures. The *response* of individuals in a market segment increases with exposure level but with diminishing returns at high levels.

Media, Exposure Levels, and Forgetting

To lay out the dimensions of the problem, let

M = number of media options under consideration.

T = number of time periods in the planning horizon.

S = number of market segments.

$$x_{jt} = \begin{cases} 1, \text{ if an insertion is made in option } j \text{ in time period } t, \\ 0, \text{ if not} \end{cases}$$

Thus, our ultimate goal will be to set the values of the x_{jt} for $j = 1, \ldots, M$ and $t = 1, \ldots, T$.

We define several terms: A *media class* will be a general means of communication, such as television, magazines, or newspapers. A *media vehicle* will be a cohesive grouping of advertising opportunities within a class, such as a particular TV show, magazine, or newspaper. A *media option* will be a detailed, purchasable unit within a vehicle. Examples would be: a commercial minute in *Bonanza,* a four-color full page in *Look,* and a half page in the Sunday *New York Times.* A *media insertion* will be a specific purchase of an option, including specification of the time period of use. A collection of insertions over a planning period will be a *media schedule.*

It is assumed that a media option: (1) is available exactly once in every time period, (2) has substantial continuity of audience, and (3) has continuity in outward format. These assumptions are for conceptual convenience and are not really very restrictive. For example, if an option cannot be available in some time period, the corresponding x_{jt} can be permanently set to zero. If the media planner wishes to permit multiple insertions of the same type in one time period, multiple media options, all alike, can be created. As much detail can be included in the specification of an option as desired; for example, a geographic area can be stipulated. Several options can be grouped together and listed as one, provided that their audiences do not appreciably overlap. Ultimately the suitability of an option depends on whether the cost, exposure, and value data described below can be provided for it.

Exposure of an individual to an insertion is taken to mean that the person has perceived the presence of the ad. A number of operational measures of exposure have been developed, different measures often being appropriate for different classes of media. The particular measures to be used in a given application are selected by the media planner.

Exposure or nonexposure of an individual to an insertion is a random variable. Consider a particular person in market segment i. Let

$$z_{ijt} = \begin{cases} 1, \text{ if the person in segment } i \text{ is exposed to an insertion in} \\ \quad \text{media option } j \text{ in period } t, \\ 0, \text{ if not.} \end{cases}$$

The probability distribution of z_{ijt} is determined by media exposure probabilities and by whether or not an insertion has been made. The arithmetic of this will be taken up below. We have been tacitly assuming that the population of interest is composed of individuals. However, for certain applications, some other basic response unit may be more appropriate and, if adopted consistently, can be used without difficulty.

We next recognize that exposures in different media options should often be assigned different values or weights. One reason is format differences. A larger ad may convey more information. (A larger ad may be more likely to be noticed too, but that effect is covered under exposure probability.) Other reasons are differences in editorial climate, mood, and reader involvement. For example, some media vehicles are thought to be supportive for certain products. An important reason is differences between media classes: An exposure to a thirty-second radio spot is to be rated on the same scale as an exposure to a half-page newspaper ad. At present, there is a large subjective element in such appraisals, but any final media schedule, however arrived at, implicitly includes such an evaluation.

The exposure weighting can be a bridge to other parts of the advertising plan. For example, the relative value of exposures in different media may be affected by the proposed communications task and copy opportunities. Thus, if a capacity for demonstrating the product is important, television would rate high. If accurate color reproduction is desirable, certain magazines would be good.

Exposure value may also differ somewhat from market segment to market segment. This seems particularly likely if market segments are defined by sex, education, or life style. Certain types of ads are routinely designed to appeal to special groups and may have much less effect on others. If such information is known in advance, it can be reflected in exposure value. Let

e_{ij} = exposure value (weight) for an exposure in media option j going to a person in market segment i (exposure value/exposure).

We must emphasize that exposure value is a property of the exposure itself and has nothing to do with cost, audience size, or exposure probability within the audience. For different options, exposure value answers the question: Given the choice of a person seeing an ad in *Life* or the same person seeing it in *Look,* does the advertiser have any preference and, if so, what is a numerical statement of that preference? For different market segments, the question is: Given that a man sees an ad in *Sports Illustrated* and that a woman sees it there, should a different weight be assigned to the exposure?

The units for exposure value are arbitrary except that they must later be tied to a response function. It is frequently convenient to conceive of an "average" media-option–market-segment combination and assign it an exposure value of 1.0. Values for other options and market segments are then assigned relative to this.

Exposure is assumed to increase a desirable quantity that will be called, simply, the *exposure level* in an individual. The amount of the increase in time period t is the weighted sum of the exposures from the insertions in the period, the weights being the exposure values.

$\sum_{j=1}^{j=M} e_{ij}z_{ijt}$ = increase in exposure level of a particular individual in market segment i in time period t (exposure value/capita).

We suppose that the effect of advertising wears off because of forgetting. Specifically, it is assumed that, in the absence of new input, exposure level decreases by a constant fraction each time period. Let

y_{it} = exposure level of a particular individual in market segment i in time period t (exposure value/capita).

α = memory constant: the fraction of y_{it} retained from one time period to the next, $0 \leq \alpha < 1$.

Then

$$y_{it} = \alpha y_{i,t-1} + \sum_{j=1}^{j=M} e_{ij}z_{ijt}. \tag{5A–1}$$

For empirical evidence on retention and decay, see Zielske[30] and Simmons.[31] If desired, the memory constant can be permitted to depend on i and t and

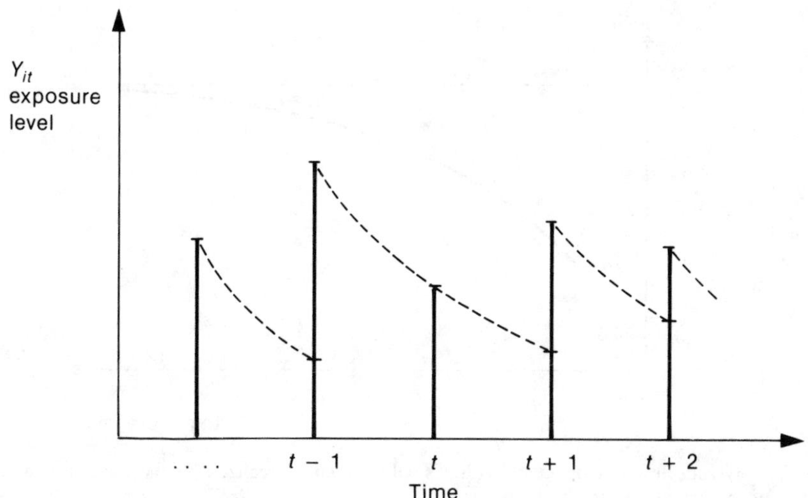

Note: Jumps represent new exposures for the time period. Dotted lines indicate forgetting between time periods.

Figure 5A–1. Exposure Level, y_{it}, over Time for Some Individual

perhaps other factors. A typical pattern of y_{it} over time might appear as in figure 5A–1.

For future reference, we note that equation 5A–1 can be rewritten as

$$y_{it} = \alpha^t y_{i,0} + \sum_{s=1}^{s=t} \sum_{j=1}^{j=M} \alpha^{t-s} e_{ij} z_{ijs},$$

or, going back indefinitely, as

$$y_{it} = \sum_{s=-\infty}^{s=t} \sum_{j=1}^{j=M} \alpha^{t-s} e_{ij} z_{ijs}. \qquad (5A\text{–}2)$$

In this form, we see that the exposure level at any point in time is a weighted sum of past exposures, with ever smaller weights being attached to ever more remote exposures. If an "average" exposure has been assigned the value of 1.0, then exposure level may be described as the number of average exposures retained at a given point in time.

Market Response

Market response is treated as follows: Each individual has a sales potential. Sales potential varies with market segment and may also be seasonal. The

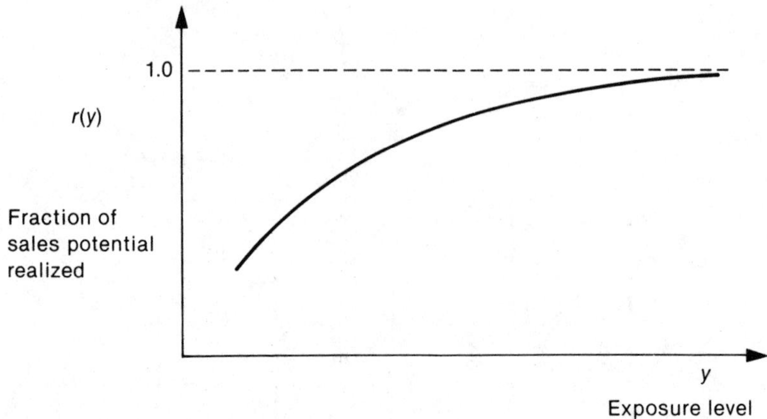

Note: The average fraction of an individual's sales potential realized by the advertiser as a function of the person's exposure level.

Figure 5A–2. Possible Response Curve

fraction of sales potential realized by an advertiser in a time period depends in a nonlinear way on the person's exposure level in that time period. Exposure level varies from individual to individual within a market segment and is described by a probability distribution. Total market response is synthesized by adding up over individuals, market segments, and time.

Specifically, let

n_i = number of people in market segment i,

w_{it} = sales potential (weight) of a person in segment i in time period t (potential units/capita/time period),

$r(y_{it})$ = response function: the fraction of potential realized when a person has exposure level y_{it},

$f_{it}(\cdot)$ = probability density of y_{it}.

The response function $r(y)$ might appear as in figure 5A–2. Let E denote the taking of expected values. Then $w_{it}E\{r(y_{it})\}$ is the average realized sales potential per person in market segment i at time t. Summing, we obtain

$$R = \sum_{i=1}^{i=S} \sum_{t=1}^{t=T} n_i w_{it} E\{r(y_{it})\}$$

$$= \text{total market response (potential units).} \qquad (5A\text{–}3)$$

The specific curve to be used for $r(y)$ will depend on the planner's judgment, and the empirical evidence available. Presumably the curve should show diminishing returns at high exposure levels. Some people feel that, at least in certain cases, the curve should show increasing returns at low levels. Others disagree; Simon[32], for example, argues that there is no empirical evidence to support increasing returns. A simple, versatile function with only diminishing returns is

$$r(y) = r_0 + a(1 - e^{-by}), \qquad (0 \leq y < \infty) \tag{5A–4}$$

where r_0, a, and b are nonnegative constants specific to the product at hand. However, our work is not restricted to this curve. Conceivably, a different function $r_{it}(y_{it})$ could be used for each i and t, but, until evidence dictates otherwise, it seems best to reflect differences between market segments and time periods simply by using sales potential as a scale factor.

The units of sales potential have not been specified. We personally tend to think of response in terms of an anticipated sales rate. Then, if sales are expressed in dollars, w_{it} has units of dollars/capita/time period and R is the expected total dollar sales to the market over the planning period. In allocating a fixed budget, however, only the shape of the response curve and the relative values of the sales potentials determine the allocation. The absolute units of the w_{it} are immaterial. Some media planners prefer to express sales potentials in arbitrary units. They feel they have a good idea of relative potentials but not of absolute potentials.

The expected response $E\{r(y_{it})\}$ for a given market segment and time period can be expressed in terms of the moments of the distribution $f_{it}(y_{it})$. Usually only the first few moments will be needed to give a good approximation to the expected response. This will turn out to be quite convenient. For notational simplicity, we drop the subscripts i and t for the present. Let

$$\mu = E\{y\} = \text{mean of } y,$$

$$\mu_n = E\{(y - \mu)^n\} = n\text{th moment of } y \text{ about the mean}, \qquad n > 1.$$

We can expand $r(y)$ in a Taylor series about μ:

$$r(y) = r(\mu) + \sum_{k=1}^{n-1} (1/k!) r^{(k)}(\mu)(y - \mu)^k + (1/n!) r^{(n)}(y_1)(y - \mu)^n, \tag{5A–5}$$

where $r^{(k)}(\mu)$ is the kth derivative of $r(y)$ evaluated at $y = \mu$ and y_1 is some value between y and μ. Taking expectations:

$$E\{r\} = r(\mu) + \sum_{k=2}^{n-1} (1/k!)r^{(k)}(\mu)\mu_k + (1/n!)E\{r^{(n)}(y_1)(y - \mu)^n\}. \quad (5A\text{–}6)$$

In practice, we would take some number of terms as our approximation and use the last term on the right to estimate the degree of approximation. Suppose, for example, we use the exponential response of (5A–4), and retain terms through the third moment. Then (5A–6) becomes

$$E\{r\} = r_0 + a(1 - e^{-b\mu}) + ae^{-b\mu}\{-(1/2)b^2\mu_2 + (1/6)b^3\mu_3\} + \epsilon_4, \quad (5A\text{–}7)$$

where $\epsilon_4 = -(1/24)aE\{e^{by_1}b^4(y - \mu)^4\}$, and $|\epsilon_4| \leq (1/24)ab^4\mu_4$, since, at most, $e^{-by_1} = 1$, and we know $(y - \mu)^4 \geq 0$.

Before leaving the response model, we observe that its conceptual generality can be broadened considerably without adding complexity. Referring back to (5A–3), we do not have to assume that everyone in a market segment actually has the same sales potential, w_{it}, nor that everybody at exposure level y responds to the same degree, $r(y)$. The quantity w_{it} can be interpreted as the average sales potential per capita in the market segment. Similarly, $r(y)$ may be viewed as a conditional expectation, the average fraction of potential realized for a group of people having the exposure level y. Both sales potential and the fraction realized may be viewed as random variables without change in (5A–3) if they are independent. If there is a basis for believing that sales potential and the fraction realized are not independent, then this basis can be used to subdivide the market segment into more homogeneous groups.

The empirical status of our construct of retained exposure level deserves comment. We do not conceive of exposure level as a directly observable property of an individual. Perhaps something close to it is observable and, if so, this would be very helpful. Quite likely, however, the communications process and the state of the individual involves a complex of quantities. If such is the case, they are deliberately aggregated here into a single index. Even if exposure level is not observable, the model can still, in principle be tested empirically. Exposures are defined operationally. The sales potentials and exposure values are prespecified numbers. Therefore, if a behavioral measure of response (say, sales) is selected, it is possible to measure inputs and outputs and fit the model to data or test it against data. Essentially we would have a problem in nonlinear regression. The difficulties in doing this are substantial, and we base our claim of utility on different grounds, but the idea remains a worthwhile possibility.

To summarize up to this point, our model deals with exposures which are assigned weights, and create an exposure level, but are gradually forgotten. The exposure level determines the fraction of a person's sales potential that is realized. Averaging over people and summing over market segments and time periods gives total response. Response can conveniently be expressed in terms of the moments of the exposure-level distribution.

Exposure Arithmetic

Our next job is to express the moments of the distribution of exposure level in terms of the media decisions, x_{jt}. The general plan is as follows: It will be shown that the mean and variance of exposure level depend only on the exposure probabilities of media singly and in pairs. Higher moments will be related to the first two. Therefore, the moments of the distribution can be calculated from exposure probability data that are not too difficult to gather and store. The exposure probabilities themselves will be developed in terms of the probability that a person is in the audience of the medium, the probability he will be exposed given that he is in the audience, and an audience seasonality factor.

Consider, for the moment, a single market segment and a single time period. We can then temporarily drop the corresponding subscripts i and t and simplify notation. Let

$$y = \text{exposure level of a particular individual,}$$

$$z_j = \begin{cases} 1, & \text{if the individual is exposed to option } j, \\ 0, & \text{if not,} \end{cases}$$

$$y = \sum_{j=1}^{j=M} e_j z_j. \tag{5A-8}$$

This expression appears to omit from y the carryover of exposure level from the previous time period, but carryover is a weighted sum of previous exposures, and just adds more terms to the sum. Let

$$p_j = P(z_j = 1) = P(\text{a person is exposed to option } j).$$

$$P_{jk} = P(z_j = 1, z_k = 1) = P(\text{a person is exposed to both option } j \text{ and option } k).$$

Thus p_j is a rating-points type of measure based on exposures, not just audience. The p_{jk} expresses the pairwise duplications. The mean of y is simply

$$E\{y\} = \sum_{j=1}^{j=M} e_j p_j. \tag{5A-9}$$

The second moment of y is

$$E\{y^2\} = E\Big\{\Big(\sum_{j=1}^{j=M} e_j z_j\Big)^2\Big\} = \sum_{j=1}^{j=M} \sum_{k=1}^{k=M} e_j e_k E\{z_j z_k\}$$

$$= \sum_{j=1}^{j=M} e_j^2 p_j + 2 \sum_{j=1}^{M-1} \sum_{k=j+1}^{k=M} e_j e_k p_{jk}, \qquad \text{(5A–10)}$$

or, letting $V(\cdot)$ denote variance,

$$V(y) = \sum_{j=1}^{j=M} e_j^2 p_j(1 - p_j) + 2 \sum_{j=1}^{M=1} \sum_{k=j+1}^{k=M} e_j e_k (p_{jk} - p_j p_k). \qquad \text{(5A–11)}$$

Equations (5A–9) and (5A–11) give us $\mu = E(y)$ and $\mu_2 = V(y)$, the first two moments of y. An expression for μ_3 can also be developed and will involve three-way overlaps among media. More generally μ_n will involve n-way overlaps. High-order overlaps are expensive to collect and expensive to store in a computer. An alternative is to estimate higher moments from lower ones. For example, the first two moments can be used to determine the parameters of an analytical probability distribution such as the gamma or log normal. Then the higher moments are implied and readily deduced. So far, however, we have not found a distribution that is computationally convenient and also fits sufficiently well to live data. It appears to be fairly easy, however, to develop empirical expressions relating higher to lower moments.

Figure 5A–3 shows plots of $\mu_n^{1/n}/\mu$ versus $\mu_2^{1/2}/\mu$ for $n = 3$ and 4 based on multiple-way audience overlap data in magazines as reported by Simmons for 1966. To form a distribution of y from such data, we must specify a set of magazines, and, for each magazine, its e_j and exposure probability for readers. In figure 5A–3, all e_js and exposure probabilities have been set to one. Each plotted point comes from a distribution of y defined by a set of magazines. As may be seen, straight lines give a good fit in the range of the data. Since $\mu_n^{1/n}/\mu$ must go to zero as $\mu_2^{1/2}/\mu$ goes to zero, we have drawn a dashed line nonlinearly back to zero. Generally, it is assumed we can determine functions

$$\mu_n = \mu_n(\mu_2, \mu). \qquad \text{(5A–12)}$$

There is a useful way to increase the accuracy of the expected response calculation (5A–6) after it has been truncated at any fixed number of moments. We observe, first, that the smaller the moments, the faster the convergence of (5A–6), and, second, that a big contributor to the size of the moments is the block of individuals who receive no exposures (have $y = 0$).

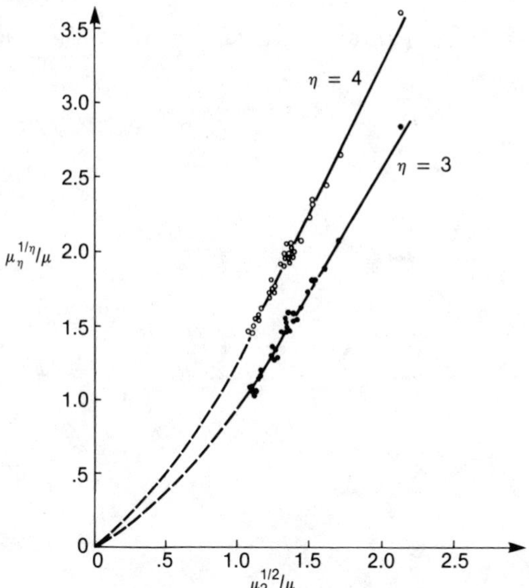

Figure 5A–3. Relating Higher Moments of the Exposure Level Distribution to the Lower

Consider, therefore, the identity

$$E\{r\} = E\{r|y = 0\}P\{y = 0\} + E\{r|y > 0\}P\{y > 0\}.$$

If we start out by calculating reach, $P\{y > 0\}$, and work out the truncated (5A–6) for the population reached, that is, $E\{r|y > 0\}$, convergence will be speeded up. Then it is straightforward to determine $E\{r|y = 1\}P\{y = 0\}$ and thence $E\{r\}$.

Next we restore time-period and market-segment subscripts by the following correspondences:

$$z_j \leftrightarrow z_{ijs},$$

$$e_j \leftrightarrow \alpha^{t-s} e_{ij},$$

$$y = \sum_{j=1}^{j=M} e_j z_j \leftrightarrow y_{it} = \sum_{s=-\infty}^{s=t} \sum_{j=1}^{j=M} \alpha^{t-s} e_{ij} z_{ijs},$$

$$p_j = P(z_j = 1) \leftrightarrow p_{j|it} = P(z_{ijt} = 1),$$

$$p_{jk} = P(z_j = 1, z_k = 1) \leftrightarrow p_{jk|its} = P(z_{ijt} = 1, z_{iks} = 1).$$

Then, using (5A–9), (5A–10), and (5A–12), we obtain moments

$$\mu_{it} = E(y_{it}) = \sum_{s=-\infty}^{s=t} \sum_{j=1}^{j=M} \alpha^{t-s} e_{ij} p_{j|is}, \tag{5A–13}$$

$$\mu_{2it} = V(y_{it}) = \sum_{s=-\infty}^{s=t} \sum_{J=1}^{j=M} (\alpha^{t-s} e_{ij})^2 p_{j|is},$$

$$+ 2 \sum_{s=-\infty}^{t-1} \sum_{r=s+1}^{r=t} \sum_{j=1}^{j=M} \sum_{k=1}^{k=M} \alpha^{t-s} e_{ij} \alpha^{t-r} e_{ik} p_{jk|isr}$$

$$+ 2 \sum_{s=-\infty}^{s=t} \sum_{j=1}^{M-1} \sum_{k=j+1}^{k=M} \alpha^{t-s} e_{ij} \alpha^{t-s} e_{ik} p_{jk|its} - \mu_{it}^2, \tag{5A–14}$$

$$\mu_{nit} = \mu_n(\mu_{2it}, \mu_{it}). \tag{5A–15}$$

The media-exposure probabilities will be modeled further. Let

$g_{j|i}$ = *market coverage* of the media vehicle of option j in segment i, defined as the fraction of people in segment i who are in the audiences of the vehicle of option j, averaged over a year.

s_{jt} = *audience seasonality,* the seasonal index for the vehicle of option j in time period t. Average value over a year is 1.0.

h_j = *exposure probability for audience member.* The probability a person is exposed to an insertion in option j given that he is in the audience of the vehicle of j.

Recalling that x_{jt} is a zero-one variable indicating presence or absence of an insertion, we take

$$p_{j|it} = g_{j|i} h_j s_{jt} x_{jt}. \tag{5A–16}$$

This expression implicitly assumes that media-vehicle seasonality can reasonably be regarded as the same in all market segments and that h_j does not change seasonally.

Next, we want the duplication probabilities, $p_{jk|its}$. These will be modeled in two steps. First, let

$$p_{jk|its} = g_{jk|i} h_j h_k s_{jt} s_{ks} x_{jt} x_{ks}, \tag{5A–17}$$

where

$g_{jk|i}$ = *segment duplication:* fraction of people in segment i who are in the audience of both the vehicle of option j and the vehicle of option k averaged over a year.

Equation (5A–17) assumes again that the h_j are not appreciably seasonal and that the events of being exposed to option j and being exposed to option k are independent, *given* that a person is in the audience of both vehicles involved. (The events of being in the audience of one vehicle and being in the audience of another are, contrary to many media models, *not* considered independent.)

The task of developing empirical tables of $g_{jk|i}$ and storing them in a computer is formidable because of the dimensionality involved. Therefore, we have developed estimating methods based on more global data.

Let

f_{jk} = fraction of the total population who are in the audience of both the vehicles of j and k, averaged over a year.

d_i = fraction of total population who are in segment i,

β = an empirically determined constant.

Then we take

$$g_{jk|i} = K_{jk}(g_{j|i}g_{k|i})^{\beta}, \qquad (5A\text{–}18)$$

where

$$K_{jk} = f_{jk} / \sum_{i=1}^{i=s} (g_{j|i}g_{k|i})^{\beta} d_i.$$

The factor K_{jk} is a normalization constant that makes segment duplications add up to global duplication. A value of 0.65 has been developed for β by fitting to 1967 vehicle-segment data in magazines as reported by Simmons. This value and the formula (5A–18) have then been tested by predicting duplications in different magazines in different segments in a different year (1968). The results are shown in figure 5A–4. The mean absolute percentage error is 10.7 percent and the mean error is 1.7 percent

Inplicitly, (5A–17) assumes that, aside from seasonality, the fraction of people who are in the audience both of vehicle A in January and of vehicle B in November is the same as the fraction who are in the audience of both vehicles in January (or November). This is probably a reasonably good assumption, but, in any case, we do not presently have any data one way or the other on the question.

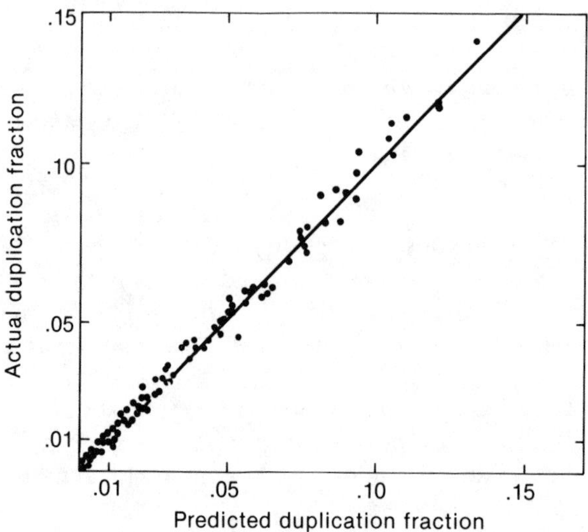

Figure 5A–4. Actual versus Predicted Audience Duplication Fraction (for Various Media Pairs in Various Market Segments

Budget Constraint

Let

c_{jt} = cost of an insertion in media option j in time t (dollars/insertion).
B = total budget for the planning period (dollars).

The budget constraint is

$$\sum_{j=1}^{j=M} \sum_{t=1}^{t=T} c_{jt} x_{jt} \leq B. \tag{5A–19}$$

The constraint is shown as linear in the number of insertions. Published rates are considerably more complex than this, and, worse yet for planning, the prices of many purchases are negotiated. From a mathematical point of view, a difficulty with many published rates is that they are neither convex nor concave. This happens when the discount for quantity applies not only to all insertions more than a fixed amount, but rather to all insertions. Then the effective cost per insertion may be zero or nearly zero in some places. For example, if an advertiser has bought eight insertions and the discount break is at nine, he might be able to get the ninth free because the use of nine insertions makes him eligible for a discount on all nine. However, heuristic methods for dealing with discounts will be developed here based on successive uses of the constraint (5A–19) with changing c_{jt}.

End Effects

The beginning and end of the planning period require special consideration. At the beginning, starting exposure levels must be specified. At the end we must find a way to evaluate advertising insertions whose effects extend beyond the planning period.

A simple and effective way to set starting exposure levels is to run the last few periods of the previous year's media schedule through the model. Ending levels for last year become starting ones for this year. Since this year's options almost always include last year's choices, the media data are readily available. If the whole previous year is run, we gain the added advantage of obtaining a comparison of the new schedule with the old under the criteria of the model.

At the other end of the planning period, we have a different problem. If we calculate response only over the planning period ($t = 1, \ldots, T$), we shall underrate the insertions during T because these also contribute to response in periods $T + 1, T + 2, \ldots$. Only if forgetting is very rapid or sales potential very small in periods right after T will there be no problem. A variety of approches can be taken to correct the situation. A few extra periods can be added after T without scheduling more insertions. This solves the underrating problem but may introduce overrating as follows: The incremental response for adding an insertion in T is composed of an increment in T, another in $T + 1$, another in $T + 2$, etc. However, the amounts of these increments depend on the exposure levels in the time periods involved. For example, high exposure levels would mean small increments because of diminishing returns. With no new insertions after T, future exposure levels will be low and the response increments may be unnaturally large. This tends to produce an overrating of the insertions in T, although the effect can be kept under control by limiting the extra periods considered.

A better but more complicated method of handling this end effect is to add extra periods but also put a schedule of new insertions into those periods. The schedule might come from various sources, but, if we are dealing with an annual plan, the most appropriate further schedule is probably a repeat of the one the model is developing. This is a little tricky, but can be done. When an insertion is put in at t, it is also put in at $t + T$. In evaluating the incremental effect of that insertion, only its placement at t is considered. However, the incremental evaluation of an insertion at T will assume the presence of the earlier insertion at both t and $t + T$.

Notationally, the end effects will be treated as follows: Let

E = the number of extra time periods added onto the end of the planning period for evaluating response.

$K + 1$ = the number of extra time periods added onto the beginning of the planning period to set starting exposure levels.

Mathematical Program

The pieces of the model can now be pulled together and the media-selection problem presented as a mathematical program. We set up the case where the objective function involves the first n terms of the Taylor expansion (5A–6) and end effects are treated by extending forward without new insertions. Provision is made for a set, I_1, of insertions that are required to be in the schedule and another set, I_2, required to be out.

MP. Find $x_{jt}(j = 1, \ldots, M;\ t = 1, \ldots, T)$ and maximal R subject to

$$R = \sum_{i=1}^{i=S} \sum_{t=1}^{T+E} n_i w_{it} \left\{ r(\mu_{it}) + \sum_{m=2}^{m=n} (1/m!) r^{(m)}(\mu_{it}) \mu_{mit} \right\}$$

$$\sum_{j=1}^{j=M} \sum_{t=1}^{t=T} c_{jt} x_{jt} \leq B,$$

$$\mu_{it} = \sum_{s=-K}^{s=t} \sum_{j=1}^{j=M} \alpha^{t-s} e_{ij} h_j g_{j|i} s_{js} x_{js},$$

$$\mu_{2it} = \sum_{s=-K}^{s=t} \sum_{j=1}^{j=M} (\alpha^{t-s} e_{ij})^2 g_{j|i} h_j s_{js} x_{js}$$

$$+ 2 \sum_{s=-K}^{t-1} \sum_{r=s+1}^{r=t} \sum_{j=1}^{j=M} \sum_{k=1}^{k=M} \alpha^{2t-r-s} e_{ij} e_{ik} g_{jk|i} h_j h_k s_{js} s_{kr} x_{js} x_{kr}$$

$$+ 2 \sum_{s=-K}^{s=t} \sum_{j=1}^{M-1} \sum_{k=j+1}^{k=M} \alpha^{2t-2s} e_{ij} e_{ik} g_{jk|i} h_j h_k s_{jt} s_{ks} x_{jt} x_{ks} - \mu_{it}^2,$$

$$\mu_{mit} = \mu_m(\mu_{it}, \mu_{2it}),\ m = 3, \ldots, n$$

$$i = 1, \ldots, S,\ t = 1, \ldots, T + E,$$

$$x_{jt} \in \{0, 1\} \text{ for all } (j, t),\ x_{jt} = 1 \text{ for } (j, t) \in I_1,\ x_{jt} = 0 \text{ for } (j, t) \in I_2.$$

Optimization

As a formal mathematical program, *MP* appears to be rather intractable. It is integer and nonlinear. Practical problems are large; for example, we have already worked on problems involving twenty media options in ten time periods, or two hundred zero-one variables. We have solved a deterministic version of the model in a one-market-segment problem by dynamic programming[28] but use of similar methods to solve *MP* does not appear reasonable.

Consequently, we have developed heuristic search methods to find schedules that are good, possibly optimal, but not necessarily guaranteed to be optimal. The basic maximum-seeking heuristic is simply that of adding to a schedule those insertions that produce a high increment of response per dollar and deleting those that produce a low decrement of response per dollar.

HS1: 1. Start with any schedule (for example, an empty one).

2. For each insertion not now in the schedule, calculate the incremental response/dollar for adding that insertion. Find the insertion with the largest value and add it to the schedule.
3. Is the budget exceeded?
   No. Return to 2.
   Yes. Continue.
4. For each insertion now in the schedule, calculate the decremental response/dollar for removal. Find an insertion with the smallest value. Call it I. Is the decrement/dollar for I greater than or equal to the increment/dollar of the most recently added insertion?
   Yes. Go to 5.
   No. Delete I. Return to 3.
5. Finish.

The above search can be expected to work well when the available insertions are not too widely different in cost and their costs are relatively small compared to the total budget. Pathological cases can be constructed and further heuristics developed to counter them, but so far the simple procedure seems to be satisfactory.

Our confidence in the basic heuristic is based on several pieces of evidence. First, a deterministic problem solved exactly by dynamic programming was solved to the same solution by the heuristic. Second, the method has always given a better solution than anyone's preconceived idea of what a schedule should be. Finally there is a theoretical reason for expecting good solutions. The objective function will usually be a concave function in the decision variables. (This might not be the case if response is strongly S-shaped, but usually expected response will be well represented by a diminishing-returns curve.) Under these circumstances, a local maximum would be a global maximum if the decision variables were continuous. As it is, they are integral, but if individual insertion costs are small compared to the budget, the solution will be likely to behave as it would in the continuous case. The importance of knowing that a local maximum is likely to be a global maximum lies in the fact that our search only explores solutions (schedules) in the immediate neighborhood of the solution currently at hand (the search tests for a local maximum). Our argument suggests that, once a local maximum is found, it is unlikely that some other, quite different solution will be better.

Since media costs are discrete numbers, the cost of the final schedule will not ordinarily equal the exact budget. The search HS1 will give a schedule that slightly exceeds the budget. By dropping out the last insertion added, the schedule can be made to fall slightly below the budget.

Consider next the problem of media discounts. A useful heuristic is to introduce media at their least cost (highest discount). If they do not appear in the schedule under these conditions, they can rather safely be ignored. If they do appear, their costs can gradually be raised to whatever value actually applies. A formal procedure is as follows:

HS2:
1. Set all costs per insertion at their lowest incremental values (that is, at the highest discount rate).
2. Solve the problem using HS1.
3. Exclude from further consideration all options not appearing in the schedule. Is the cost of each option entered at its actual average cost per insertion (including discounts) for the current schedule?
   Yes. Go to step 5.
   No. Continue.
4. Find the option with the largest discrepancy between the actual average cost per insertion for the current schedule and the cost being used. For this option(s) put in the actual average cost. Return to step 2.
5. Finish.

The search is operated off-line except for step 2. Visual inspection is often used to skip steps and save computing time. HS2 is probably not as good as HS1. The possibility of multiple local maxima seems intuitively more severe.

Data Considerations

The job of supplying inputs is left to the user. Some people have claimed that, if they had all the needed data, the best schedule would be obvious. Experience contradicts this, but an important sidelight on the model is that users often gain valuable insights in the course of assembling the data. It is also true that gathering the inputs usually takes considerable effort. The purpose of this section is to indicate that the obstacles involved are surmountable, although we make no pretense of covering all situations.

A complete list of input requirements is given in the appendix. Certain items are straightforward. They have been developed many times before, and the conceptual and measurement problems are minimal. In this category we put most market-segment data, such as definition, population, sales potential, and seasonality. In constructing sales potentials, it is well to remember the use to which the numbers are to be put. For example, if a branded product shows wide regional variations in level of distribution and this situation is fairly stable, a realistic sales potential for the model would be high where distribution is high, and low where distribution is low.

Media data that are reasonably straightforward include the list of media options, market-segment coverage for each vehicle, the cost per insertion, the probability of exposure to the option for a member of the audience of the vehicle, and audience duplication between pairs of vehicles. It is expected that audience duplication data may only be available for the total population, but, as previously indicated, it can usually be broken down by individual market segments through empirical estimating equations. Upper bounds on the number of insertions are generally the result of physical limitations on the number of issues, shows, etc., available in the one time period. Policy restrictions may also enter. Ordinarily it seems desirable to let the model optimize freely without arbitrary constraints, but realistically these exist and, in addition, by permitting them in the model, one can test them for their effect on the solution.

Media and market-segment data are often pieced together from a variety of sources. One important source for consumer products is a national survey in which people are simultaneously interviewed as to demographic characteristics, product use, and media habits. National surveys, however, may yield rather small samples for individual market areas and for local or relatively rare, but possibly efficient, media. Sometimes a fruitful approach is to survey high-potential groups directly to uncover the media they use. Recently, a good deal of work has been done on clustering and nonmetric scaling. This may be quite helpful in defining meaningful market segments.

The more difficult inputs are the exposure values for the various media, the memory constant, and the individual response function.

The setting of the exposure values can be broken into three parts: (1) the setting of relative values among broad media classes, such as TV, magazines, and newspapers; (2) an adjustment for individual vehicles or options within a media class (such as *Life, Look,* and *Newsweek*); and (3) an adjustment for market segment (men, women, and children, for example). The latter two parts are usually handled judgmentally and often represent rather small adjustments. (Recall that exposure value has nothing to do with cost, exposure probability, or sales potential, but rather with whether it is preferred to have a person see an ad in one vehicle or another and whether it is thought that an exposure will have a greater effect on a person in one market segment or another in terms of increasing his percent of potential realized.)

For setting relative values among media classes, an "economic equilibrium" approach can be useful. First, a portfolio of media options is formed for each media class. The portfolio is a sample from the principal vehicles that advertisers use. Then, on the basis of some standard space unit for the class (such as black-and-white full pages in magazines), a cost per thousand exposures is calculated for the class. Next it is assumed that economic forces tend approximately to equalize the value obtained from different media classes when taken as a whole. Under this hypothesis, exposure value is proportional to the reciprocal of cost per thousand. Some class can be assigned the value 1.0 and then the values for other classes are calculated.

Notice that use of this method does not imply that all media classes will be equally attractive to a given advertiser. He will have his own circumstances, particularly with respect to market segmentation, sales potential, and media coverage of the segments. In addition, he may have special communications opportunities in a certain media class because of the particular needs of his product, and these may lead him to adjust the exposure value for the class.

With respect to the memory constant and individual response, a certain number of empirical studies have been published. Zielske[30] displays data on recall versus time, as does a more recent Simmons report.[31] A BBDO booklet[33] summarizes several studies and gives a bibliography. Examples of published work displaying diminishing-returns phenomena are Benjamin and Maitland,[2] who measure the effect of advertising on sales, and Rohloff,[34] who measures pre–post brand-choice scores. These studies tend to support the basic concepts of the model and offer insight into the range of effects to be expected. When it comes to setting values for a specific application, we have generally found that media planners are able to make judgmental estimates of the needed quantities. To aid the process we have evolved a short series of questions about response. (See computer trace in table 5A–2.) The answers are then used to develop a response function. As with any other part of the input, if the user feels the values are known only within a range, he can make runs with different values to test the sensitivity of the results.

Some companies are fortunate enough to have performed field experiments that measure the effect of advertising exposures or expenditures on sales. Such measurements can be used to calibrate the model. The particular way of doing this will depend on how the experimental results are presented, but, to illustrate, suppose that the measurements indicate that a 10-percent increase in advertising spending would result in a specified sales increase and that a 10-percent decrease in spending would produce a specified sales decrease under the conditions of last year's media schedule. Then, using last year's schedule and all the model parameters except the response function, one can use the model to calculate exposure levels in each market segment and also levels 10 percent higher and lower. Then the parameters of the response function can be determined so that the model-calculated results match the experimental values at the given points. When calibrated in this way, the model makes an allocation that is consistent with the company's best information about sales response.

MEDIAC: An On-Line Media Selection System

The model and heuristics have been implemented on a time-shared computer. This permits a close interaction between user and model. In particular, the user obtains immediate on-line access from a remote terminal, English-language communication, and self-explaining operation. Working with the system on-line gives the media planner an intuitive feel for the behavior of the model and the selection process that is difficult to obtain otherwise. The model becomes not a mysterious black box, but a routine tool that acts in rather ordinary and expectable ways.

A major advantage of time-sharing is that an organization with relatively low total computer usage can gain access to a powerful machine without incurring the elaborate overhead in personnel, space, and cost that usually accompanies big machines. The computer used for the following example is an SDS 940 at a commercial time-sharing firm.

We have called the on-line system MEDIAC. Its principal capabilities currently include: input, data storage, data alteration, schedule evaluation, schedule selection, and output. With respect to size, we have solved a problem with 24 media options, 10 time periods, and 15 market segments, and substantially larger problems are feasible.

MEDIAC presently uses an exponential response function of the form (4) with $r_0 = 0$. The a and b are fit to the answers from the response questions. Two moments are used in the Taylor series. Added accuracy is obtained by breaking off a block of population not reached, as discussed in the section on exposure arithmetic. End effects are treated by extending the planning horizon two periods and assuming that the schedule being developed will be repeated. The optimization heuristic presently adds insertions but does not delete them.

The operation of MEDIAC is best demonstrated by example. A sample problem is worked out in detail below. The problem involves four media, eight time periods, and two market segments. A summary of all input data is given in table 5A–1. Detailed definitions of the data categories may be found in the appendix. The data are completely hypothetical. (We had originally planned to show a problem whose output has been implemented but it would take up too much space.)

The transcript of the on-line computer session is shown in table 5A–2. The system has a number of features not demonstrated here. For example, the data can conveniently be stored, changed, and printed out. A preliminary

Table 5A–1
Data for Sample Problem

PRODUCT: 'MINI-WIDGETS'

Budget: $350,000 | *Time Periods: Weeks (8)*

Media options (4):	60-sec TV Program *A*	60-sec TV Program *B*	4-color page Magazine *A*	4-color page Magazine *B*
Cost/insertion	$18,000	$45,000	$26,000	$10,000
Exposure probability for audience member	0.4	0.4	0.5	0.3
Exposure value	2.0	2.5	1.5	0.75

Upper bounds: 1 insertion/period for each media option
Audience seasonality: none

Market segments (2):	Men over 20	Women over 20
Population (000)	45,000	50,000
Sales potential ($/person/week)	0.05	0.14
Seasonality	none	none
Initial exposure value	0	0

Memory constant: 0.7

Percent potential realized:

at saturation	100
at 1 average exposure	50
at 2 average exposures	70
at 3 average exposures	80

Market Coverage:

	Men	*Women*
TV *A*	0.01	0.12
TV *B*	0.25	0.18
Mag *A*	0.20	0.12
Mag *B*	0.01	0.17

Media Vehicle Duplication:

	TV A	*TV B*	*Mag A*	*Mag B*
TV *A*	0.030	0.020	0.030	0.020
TV *B*		0.110	0.070	0.020
Mag *A*			0.060	0.020
Mag *B*				0.080

ranking of media options can be made. It is based on using single insertions in isolation, and offers insight into why a schedule comes out as it does.

Discussion

We have presented a calculus for selecting advertising media, that is, a system of numerical procedures for transforming data and judgments into a media schedule. The goal has been to develop a tool for today, an improvement in the state of the art relative to present practice. Our calculus uses data that

Table 5A–2
Running the Sample Problem On-Line at a Teletype Computer Terminal

```
→ PLEASE LOG IN: G3;A121;
  READY  11/11  2Ø:Ø2
→ -GO (G2AØ11) /@INPUT/

  TYPE NO. OF DOLLARS IN BUDGET,F9.
→ 35ØØØØ.,
  TYPE THE NO. OF TIME PERS,I3
→ 8,
  TYPE NO. OF MKT SEGMENTS,I3
→ 2,
  TYPE NO. OF MEDIA,I4
→ 4,
  TYPE THE PERCENT OF POTENTIAL REALIZED
  AFTER COMPLETE SATURATION WITH EXPOSURES,F4
→ 1ØØ.,
  TYPE PERCENT OF POTENTIAL REALIZED
  AFTER 1AVERAGE EXPOSURES/CAPITA,F4.
→ 5Ø.,
  TYPE PERCENT OF POTENTIAL REALIZED
  AFTER 2AVERAGE EXPOSURES/CAPITA,F4.
→ 7Ø.
  TYPE PERCENT OF POTENTIAL REALIZED
  AFTER 3AVERAGE EXPOSURES/CAPITA,F4.
→ 8Ø.
  TYPE NAME OF MKT SEG    1 A6
→ MEN...
  TYPE NO. OF PEOPLE,POTENTIAL FOR SEGMENT MEN...,2F9
→ 45ØØØ.,.Ø5,
  TYPE NAME OF MKT SEG    2 A6
→ WOMEN.
  TYPE NO. OF PEOPLE,POTENTIAL FOR SEGMENT WOMEN.,2F9
→ 5ØØØØ.,.14,
  TYPE MEMORY CONSTANT,F4.
→ .7,
  TYPE NAME OF MEDIA    1 A6
→ TVA...
  TYPE EXPOSURE VALUE,PROG. OF EXPOSURE,2F3.,OF TVA...
→ 2.Ø,.4,
  TYPE NAME OF MEDIA    2 A6
→ TVB...
  TYPE EXPOSURE VALUE,PROB. OF EXPOSURE,2F3.,OF TVB...
→ 2.5,.4,
  TYPE NAME OF MEDIA    3 A6
→ MAGA..
  TYPE EXPOSURE VALUE,PROB. OF EXPOSURE,2F3.,OF MAGA..
→ 1.5,.5,
  TYPE NAME OF MEDIA    4 A6
→ MAGB..
  TYPE EXPOSURE VALUE,PROB. OF EXPOSURE,2F3.,OF MAGB..
→ .75,.3,
  IF THERE IS NO MEDIA SEASONALITY,TYPE 1,OTHERWISE 2
→ 1,
  IF SEG. COVER. OF MOST MEDIA IS Ø.,TYPE 1,ELSE2
→ 2,
  TYPE MKT.SEG.COVERAGE OF TVA... SEGMENTS
  MEN.WOME
  .XXX.XXX
→ .Ø1Ø.12Ø
```

Lines marked → contain typing done by user. The rest was typed back by the computer (except for these explanatory notes).

User calls INPUT program to begin generating data bank. The computer asks for all data needed. The F, I, and A letters refer to input format.

are available or procurable along with those judgments that seem essential to define a solution. The on-line computer system is fast, easy to use, and inexpensive relative to the importance of the problem and other models of comparable scope.

There are some things the model is and some it is not. It *is* an allocation model; that is, it takes a fixed budget and spreads it over time and market

Table 5A–2 (continued)

```
    TYPE MKT.SEG.COVERAGE OF TVB... SEGMENTS
    MEN.WOME
    .XXX.XXX
→   .25Ø.18Ø
    TYPE MKT.SEG.COVERAGE OF MAGA.. SEGMENTS
    MEN.WOME
    .XXX.XXX
→   .2ØØ.12Ø
    TYPE MKT.SEG.COVERAGE OF MAGB.. SEGMENTS
    MEN.WOME
    .XXX.XXX
→   .Ø1Ø.17Ø
    TYPE COST PER INSERT F6, FOR TVA...
→   18ØØØ.,
    TYPE COST PER INSERT F6, FOR TVB...
→   45ØØØ.,
    TYPE COST PER INSERT F6, FOR MAGA..
→   26ØØØ.,
    TYPE COST PER INSERT F6, FOR MAGB..
→   1ØØØØ.,
    TYPE NO OF SEGS WITH SEASONAL POTENTIAL
→   Ø,
    TYPE NO. OF CASES(PERIODS*MEDIA) WITH
    UPPER BOUNDS NOT EQUAL TO ONE
→   Ø,
    TYPE1 IF DUPLS ARE AVAI, 2MEANS INDEPENDENC
→   1,
    TYPE 1 IF DUPS ARE STORED,OTHERWISE 2
→   2,
    TYPE DUPLICATIONS OF TVA... WITH
    TVA.TVB.MAGAMAGB
    .XXX.XXX.XXX.XXX
→   .Ø3Ø.Ø2Ø.Ø3Ø.Ø2Ø
    TYPE DUPLICATIONS OF TVB... WITH
    TVB.MAGAMAGB
    .XXX.XXX.XXX
→   .11Ø.Ø7Ø.Ø2Ø
    TYPE DUPLICATIONS OF MAGA.. WITH
    MAGAMAGB
    .XXX.XXX
→   .Ø6Ø.Ø2Ø
    TYPE DUPLICATIONS OF MAGB.. WITH
    MAGB
    .XXX
→   .Ø8Ø
```

The data bank for the problem is now created. It can be changed, printed out, discarded, or stored indefinitely as desired.

The user calls for the MEDIAC main program which will develop a schedule from the above data.

```
    *STOP*

    +
→   -GO (G2AØ11) /@MEDIAC/
```

```
    TYPE 1 IF INITIAL EXPOSURES ARE ZERO, OTHERWISE 2
→   1,
    TYPE 1 FOR RANKING, OTHERWISE 2
→   2,
    TYPE 1 IF SOME MEDIA HAVE ALREADY BEEN SELECTED, OTHERWISE 2
→   2,
```

Initial exposure zero would be appropriate for a new product.

segments. It is *not,* however, a budgeting model. If market response is expressed as sales, the model appears to be capable of determining an optimal advertising budget. Such a use is unwarranted unless the model has been calibrated on sales response data. The reason is that although the allocation of a fixed budget depends on the shape of the response curve, it will be fairly insensitive to modest changes and will be completely insensitive to changes in scale factor. On the other hand, the optimal budget will be quite sensitive to such changes. For example, if the response function were multiplied by a

Table 5A–2 (continued)

```
MAGA.. TIME PER  1 COST    26ØØØ.REALIZED POT.      14Ø7.
MAGA.. TIME PER  6 COST    52ØØØ.REALIZED POT.      2529.
MAGA.. TIME PER  3 COST    78ØØØ.REALIZED POT.      376Ø.
MAGB.. TIME PER  1 COST    88ØØØ.REALIZED POT.      4192.
MAGB.. TIME PER  5 COST    98ØØØ.REALIZED POT.      4571.
MAGA.. TIME PER  2 COST   124ØØØ.REALIZED POT.      5712.
MAGA.. TIME PER  7 COST   15ØØØØ.REALIZED POT.      6567.
MAGB.. TIME PER  2 COST   16ØØØØ.REALIZED POT.      6939.
MAGA.. TIME PER  4 COST   186ØØØ.REALIZED POT.      79Ø6.
MAGB.. TIME PER  6 COST   196ØØØ.REALIZED POT.      82Ø9.
MAGB.. TIME PER  3 COST   2Ø6ØØØ.REALIZED POT.      8533.
MAGA.. TIME PER  5 COST   232ØØØ.REALIZED POT.      9362.
MAGB.. TIME PER  7 COST   242ØØØ.REALIZED POT.      9611.
MAGB.. TIME PER  4 COST   252ØØØ.REALIZED POT.      9886.
TVB... TIME PER  1 COST   297ØØØ.REALIZED POT.     11399.
TVA... TIME PER  1 COST   315ØØØ.REALIZED POT.     11889.
MAGB.. TIME PER  8 COST   325ØØØ.REALIZED POT.     12Ø87.
TVB... TIME PER  6 COST   37ØØØØ.REALIZED POT.     13Ø73.
```

The schedule is printed out as it is developed by the computer. MAGA is best at first, but duplication with itself and diminishing returns soon bring in other media which cover different people.

```
MEDIAC GENERATED SCHEDULE

MEDIA  PER.  1    2    3    4    5    6    7    8
TVA...       X
TVB...       X                        X
MAGA..       X    X    X    X    X    X    X
MAGB..       X    X    X    X    X    X    X    X
```

The schedule is heavy in the first period because initial exposure level was zero.

```
TYPE 1 FOR DETAILED Ø/P,ELSE 2
1,
SEGMENT TIME P EX VAL/CP SEG E.V.      REALIZED POTENTIAL
  MEN...     1   .4Ø957   18431.          215.
  MEN...     2   .43873   19743.          299.
  MEN...     3   .45913   2Ø661.          343.
  MEN...     4   .47342   213Ø4.          368.
  MEN...     5   .48342   21754.          382.
  MEN...     6   .74Ø17   333Ø8.          448.
  MEN...     7   .67Ø14   3Ø156.          466.
  MEN...     8   .47127   212Ø7.          4Ø1.
  MEN...     9   .32989   14845.          329.
  MEN...    1Ø   .23Ø92   1Ø392.          254.
  WOMEN.     1   .4Ø357   2Ø179.          649.
  WOMEN.     2   .41Ø53   2Ø526.          862.
  WOMEN.     3   .41539   2Ø77Ø.          966.
  WOMEN.     4   .4188Ø   2Ø94Ø.         1Ø16.
  WOMEN.     5   .42119   21Ø59.         1Ø41.
  WOMEN.     6   .6Ø26Ø   3Ø13Ø.         1151.
  WOMEN.     7   .54985   27492.         12Ø4.
  WOMEN.     8   .423Ø7   21153.         1112.
  WOMEN.     9   .29615   148Ø7.          917.
  WOMEN.    1Ø   .2Ø73Ø   1Ø365.          71Ø.
```

The detailed output shows level of retained exposure value per capita, total retained exposure value, and total realized potential for each segment in each time period.

Total time for the run including a data printout and media ranking not shown was less than thirty minutes at the terminal.

large constant, the allocation would not change but the optimal budget would change substantially.

We have in mind a number of extensions of MEDIAC. These include the effect of competitive advertising, the rub-off effect of other advertising by the same firm, and the possibility of certain synergistic effects. Undoubtably, still others will be developed.

Experience with MEDIAC has been very encouraging. Several million dollars of advertising have been scheduled and implemented in the few months that the system has been operational. Although we have found some people who do not want to quantify their media decisions, we have found a growing number who find the system a distinct aid. Improvements in the objective functions, as defined by the users, have ranged from about 5 percent to 25 percent relative to previous schedules. Some MEDIAC-computed schedules have looked much like previous ones; others have been quite different. In cases that have looked different, it has been possible to find out what data or phenomena have caused the change. So far the media planner has invariably preferred the new schedule.

How has the use of MEDIAC affected the way users think about their media planning decisions? Perhaps the most important contribution is the introduction of a relatively comprehensive problem structure. People often show a tendency to pick out one or two important issues of a problem and let these make the decision. The model leads people to look at many issues and ferret out information on all of them. The model then interrelates the information in a unified way. Usually, a relatively few numbers are in fact the key determinants of the decision, but not always are they the numbers thought in advance to be important.

MEDIAC seems to move the intuitive approach of the media planner to a more productive level. More effort goes into formulating the problem than into trying to perceive the answer in one jump. Not that users automatically accept the model's answers; they test the answers against their intuition, dig into the model to find out what caused any discrepancies and, in the process, appear to be updating and enriching their intuition.

Appendix

MEDIAC Input

I. *Media characteristics:* Data needed for each media option.

1. Name of option.
2. Cost per insertion.
3. Exposure probability for audience member. The probability a person is exposed to the particular ad in the vehicle given that he is in the audience of the vehicle.
4. Upper bounds on insertions. The maximum number of times the media option can be used in each time period.
5. Audience seasonality. The audience size for each time period for the media vehicle, expressed as an index with an average value of 1.0.
6. Exposure value. Exposure value answers the following type of question: Given the choice of a person seeing an ad in *Life* or the same person seeing it in *Look,* does the advertiser have any preference, and, if so, what is the statement of that preference? It is usual to con-

ceive of an average media option and assign it to a value of 1.0 and then assign values for other media options relative to it.

II. *Market characteristics:* Data needed for each market segment.

1. Name of segment.
2. Population.
3. Sales potential per person in the segment. The units of sales potential are chosen by the user.
4. Seasonality of sales potential. This is an index with a value for each time period in the advertising plan plus two time periods for ending effects. The average value over a full year is 1.00.
5. Initial average exposure value per person in the segment. As a substitute for this data, a list of the media insertions planned for two months before the computer-generated schedule is to start will suffice.

III. *Media-segment data*

1. Market coverage. For each media vehicle in each segment, the fraction of the segment population who will be in the audience of the media vehicle. Essentially, this amounts to rating points in the market segment.

IV. *Media-vehicle duplications*

1. Audience duplication. For each possible pair of media vehicles the fraction of people out of the total in all segments who will be in the audience of both vehicles. Also needed is the fraction of people who will be in the audience of two appearances of the vehicle. If duplication data are not available, the system can approximate them using the assumption of independence between media.

V. *Other data needed*

1. Memory constant. The fraction of a person's exposure value that is remembered from one time period to the next.
2. The percent of potential realized after saturation with exposures.
3. The percent of potential realized when one, two, and three average exposures are retained by a person. (An average exposure is defined as an exposure to a media option with exposure value of 1.0.) These inputs may be viewed as expressing the expected effect of having one, two, and three exposures presented to a person in a short period of time. When combined with the saturation level, these inputs determine the diminishing returns aspect of response.
4. Number of media options, market segments, and time periods.
5. Budget.

References

1. M.L. Vidale and H.B. Wolfe, "An Operations Research Study of Sales Response to Advertising," *Operations Research* 5 (1957):370–81.

2. B. Benjamin and J. Maitland, "Operational Research and Advertising: Some Experiments in the Use of Analogies," *Operational Research Quarterly* 9 (1958): 207–17.

3. R.A. Metheringham, "Measuring the Net Cumulative Coverage of a Print Campaign," *Journal of Advertising Research* 4 (December 1964):23–28.

4. D.W. Miller and M.K. Starr, *Executive Decisions and Operations Research* (Englewood Cliffs, N.J.: Prentice–Hall, 1960).

5. C.L. Wilson, "Use of Linear Programming to Optimize Media Schedules in Advertising" in *Proceedings of the Forty-Sixth National Conference of the American Marketing Association,* ed. H. Gomez (Chicago: American Marketing Association, 1963).

6. R.D. Buzzell, *Mathematical Models and Marketing Management* (Boston: Harvard University, Graduate School of Business Administration, 1964), chap. 5.

7. R.L. Day, "Linear Programming in Media Selection," *Journal of Advertising Research* 2 (June 1962):40–44.

8. J.F. Engel and M.R. Warshaw, "Allocating Advertising Dollars by Linear Programming," *Journal of Advertising Research* 4 (September 1964):42–48.

9. S.F. Stasch, "Linear Programming and Space–Time Considerations in Media Selection," *Journal of Advertising Research* 5 (December 1965):40–46.

10. F.M. Bass and R.T. Lonsdale, "An Exploration of Linear Programming in Media Selection," *Journal of Marketing Research* 3 (1966):179–88.

11. P. Kotler, "Toward an Explicit Model for Media Selection," *Journal of Advertising Research* 4 (March 1964):34–41.

12. M.L. Godfrey, "Media Selection by Mathematical Programming." Talk before the Metropolitan New York chapter of the Institute of Management Sciences, October 10, 1962.

13. D.B. Brown and M.R. Warshaw, "Media Selection by Linear Programming," *Journal of Marketing Research* 2 (1965):83–88.

14. W.I. Zangwill, "Media Selection by Decision Programming," *Journal of Advertising Research* 5 (September 1965):30–36.

15. A. Charnes, W.W. Cooper, J.K. DeVoe, D.B. Learner, and W. Reinecke, *LP II: A Goal Programming Model for Media Planning,* Management Sciences Research Report no. 96 (Pittsburgh: Carnegie Institute of Technology, Graduate School of Industrial Administration, January 1967).

16. "Simulmatics Media-Mix Technical Description" (New York: Simulmatics Corporation, October 1962).

17. W.T. Moran, "Practical Media Models—What Must They Look Like" in *Proc. 8th Conference of the Advertising Res. Foundation* (New York: 1962).

18. D.B. Brown, "A Practical Procedure for Media Selection," *Journal of Marketing Research* 4 (1967):262–64.

19. D.H. Gensch, "A Computer Simulation Model for Media Selection," Ph.D. dissertation (Evanston, Ill.: Northwestern University, 1967).

20. A.M. Lee and A.J. Burkart, "Some Optimization Problems in Advertising Media Planning," *Operational Research Quarterly* 11 (1960):113–22.

21. C.J. Taylor, "Some Developments in the Theory and Application of Media Scheduling Methods," *Operational Research Quarterly* 14 (1963):291–305.

22. A.M. Lee, "Decision Rules for Media Scheduling: Static Campaigns," *Operational Research Quarterly* 13 (1962):229–42.

23. ———, "Decision Rules for Media Scheduling: Dynamic Campaigns," *Operational Research Quarterly* 14 (1963):355–72.

24. D.M. Ellis, "Building up a Sequence of Optimum Media Schedules," *Operational Research Quarterly* 17 (1966):413–24.

25. E.M.L. Beale, P.A.B. Hughes, and S.R. Broadbent, "A Computer Assessment of Media Schedules," *Operational Research Quarterly* 17 (1966):381–412.

26. N. Steinberg, G. Comes, and J. Barache, "Un Modèele de Simulation pour Evaluer l'Efficacite d' un Plan de Supports" in *The Fourth International Conference on Operational Research: Preprints of the Proceedings,* B60–66 (Boston: 1966).

27. P. Bertier and P. duJeu, "Simulation des Comportements Aléeatoires de Lecture: Le Modèele Scal," *Metra* 6:647–59.

28. J.D.C. Little and L.M. Lodish, "A Media Selection Model and Its Optimization by Dynamic Programming," *Industrial Management Review* 8 (1966):15–24.

29. G. Franzi, "Mathematical Programming and Media Selection in Advertising," S.M. thesis (Cambridge: MIT, January 1967).

30. H.A. Zielske, "The Remembering and Forgetting of Advertising," *Journal of Marketing* 23 (1959):239–43.

31. "A Study of the Retention of Advertising in Five Magazines" (New York: W.R. Simmons & Associates Research, 1965).

32. J.L. Simon, "Are There Economies of Scale in Advertising?" *Journal of Advertising Research* 5 (June 1965):15–20.

33. D.B. Learner, "Repetition of Advertising" (New York: Batten, Barton, Durstine, and Osborne research department, February 1967).

34. A.C. Rohloff, "Quantitative Analysis of the Effectiveness of TV Commercials," *Journal of Marketing Research* 3 (1966):239–45.

35. S. Banks, "Use of Incremental Analysis in the Selection of Advertising Media," *Journal of Business* 19 (1946):232–43.

6
Television: Viewing Choice Models, Ratings Models, and Program Scheduling Models

This chapter highlights recent developments in modeling television viewing. In contrast to previous chapters, not all of the models presented here will be directly applicable to the problems of advertisers and advertising agencies.

Viewing choice models refer to models of how an individual chooses between several viewing options at a particular point in time. Such models attempt to capture determinants of individual behavior. Understanding viewing choice at the individual level is indispensable for determining the probable effect of program schedule changes, and as a basis for building ratings prediction models.

Ratings models attempt to predict the ratings that will be achieved by particular programs. This turns out to be a difficult undertaking, and only a good understanding of individual viewing choice will enable the building of acceptable models.

Program scheduling models are models that seek to guide a television network (or station) in choosing the best times at which to air particular programs.

Viewing Choice Models

Viewing choice may be described at either the aggregate level or the individual level. Aggregate models of viewing choice are termed ratings models, and are dealt with in the next section. Individual level viewing choice is a subject that has not been considered in depth until relatively recently, and there is considerable room for further research in the area.

Ironically, one of the most interesting findings concerning individual viewing choice is the implication of research concerning aggregate choice. Gensch and Shaman showed that the total audience watching network television at any time is highly predictable, *regardless of program content.*[6,7] This implies that viewing is for most people a two-step process. The first step is to turn the television on, and the second step is to choose the best available program.

Thus the traditional image of people who turn on the television expressly to watch particular favorite programs is seriously questioned. Instead we are left with an image of "couch potatoes" choosing the "least objectionable alternative."

The Rust–Alpert Audience Flow Model

The two-step process of viewing choice provides the basis for the Rust–Alpert audience flow viewing choice model.[17] This model incorporates the concepts of economic utility, audience flow, and audience segmentation to produce a model that can be used to predict individual viewing choice, and also, by extension, to predict ratings and ratings changes. This article is reprinted at the end of the chapter.

The Luce axiom provides the framework for how economic utility theory translates to viewing choice.[15,16] The idea is that, for a particular individual, each viewing option (possible program to be viewed) has a certain amount of utility associated with it. However there is also disutility involved. For example, getting up to change channels involves a certain amount of disutility. This is actually measurable, as will be seen later! The Rust–Alpert model sets up in a mathematical framework the major sources of utility and disutility affecting the individual viewing choice.

Let us denote the utility of viewing half-hour program segment (viewing option) v to individual i as $u(i,v)$, with corresponding probability of choice $c(i,v)$. Consistent with the Luce axiom, we assume that the probability of individual i viewing half-hour program segment v^*, given that he or she has chosen to watch television that half hour, is

$$c(i,v^*) = u(i,v,^*)/\sum u(i,v) \tag{6.1}$$

where the sum is over all of the viewing options in the same time slot.

It would be impossible to model these utilities separately for every individual in the population. Thus a simplifying assumption is used. The population is broken up into segments assumed to have the same utilities, given the same viewing situation. For the purpose of research, the segments were formed on the basis of age, education, and sex, although the model is general enough to permit any segmentation scheme.

As in previous chapters, television programs are assumed to belong to a particular program type. The same program type classification is used throughout this book, although other program type classifications (such as the Nielsen NTI classification) could just as easily be used. A distinct set of program type utilities is assumed for each segment. This is to reflect the tendency for some segments to like particular types of programs better than others. For example, it will be seen that the male segments have a positive utility for sports programs.

A central and unique part of the model is the assumption of six "flow states" which may affect the utility of a viewing option. These are detailed in the reprinted article. A separate flow state exists for each combination of individual and viewing option in a particular half-hour period. The flow state incorporates information as to whether the television was (in the previous half hour) on or off. If the set was on, the flow state incorporates whether it was tuned to the same channel on which the viewing option is appearing, and whether or not the viewing option is the continuation of a program already in progress. To reduce computation, the utilities derived from these flow states are assumed to be constant across the segments, although this assumption could easily be relaxed.

The utility to individual i of viewing option v may be considered an average utility plus a deviation from the average. The model then uses the variables just described to predict this deviation. The form of this prediction model is regression with effect coded variables.[12] Effect coding is a variation of dummy variable coding which allows interpretations similar to that of analysis of variance.

There are undoubtedly other model forms which might be used, within the same general theoretical framework. One of the reasons this one was used is that it is easily implemented on standard statistical packages, using a regression subprogram.

The flow state variable **F** is a vector corresponding to viewing option v and individual i, which reflects whether the television was previously on or off; if it was on, whether it was tuned to the same channel as v; and whether v is the start or continuation of a program. For example (from table 6A–2), if the set has just been turned on, and viewing option v is the start of a program, then flow state 5 applies.

The program type variable **T** is a vector corresponding to viewing option v and individual i, which reflects the segment of individual i and the program type of viewing option v.

Using the variables described above, it is possible to express concisely the utility of viewing option v to individual i,

$$u(i,v,) = \mu + \mathbf{B}_1\mathbf{F} + \mathbf{B}_2\mathbf{T} + e_{iv} \tag{6.2}$$

where μ is the overall unweighted mean utility across the groups defined by variables **F** and **T**, e_{iv} represents the unexplained deviation (assumed to be normally distributed), and $\mathbf{B}_1$ and $\mathbf{B}_2$ are coefficient vectors.

This formulation looks simple, but the estimation of the Rust–Alpert audience flow model is subtly complex. For the details of the estimation of the model, the reader is referred to the following reprinted article.

The model was tested on 1977 Simmons data. The results of the coefficient estimates are quite interesting, and are shown in the reprinted article. By the end of the iterative estimation procedure, the R^2 had reached .93, suggesting good explanatory ability.

All coefficients are of the sign and relative magnitude anticipated. For example, the second flow state has a large positive coefficient. This flow state corresponds to a situation in which the set is already on and tuned to the right channel, while the viewing option represents the continuation of a program; for example, someone is in the middle of watching a program. It seems reasonable to associate a relatively high utility with the program's continuation.

The program type coefficients are also as expected. For example, the highest utility increment is associated with the combination of young, educated men and sports programming. It is also interesting, and entirely expected, that all of the female segments have a negative utility deviation associated with sports.

The predictive ability of the model was tested using prime-time programs on Wednesday and Friday. These days were chosen in an attempt to pick typical days of the week while minimizing overlap with the programs used to estimate the model. Different weeks were used, to further maximize the difference between the estimation programs and the validation programs. There were 12 half-hour time slots used in the validation, involving 30 viewing options and 19,050 individual viewing choices.

The prediction of the model was compared to actual choice, for each individual, for each choice occasion. The model predicted viewing choice correctly 76 percent of the time (corresponding to a mean prediction error of two rating points).

Other Viewing Choice Models

An economic utility approach was used previously by Lehmann to predict preference of television programs.[13] His model did not take the extra step of predicting choice. Darmon constructed a model which related viewing choice to program type and channel loyalty,[3] and Zufryden used a linear learning model approach which assumed inertia of choice across choice occasions.[19]

Bower,[2] Villani,[18] and Frank and Greenberg[4,5] have all investigated viewing choice, especially as it relates to particular viewer segments. However much of the most interesting and well-developed work in this area has been done in England by Goodhardt, Ehrenberg, Barwise, and Collins.

An interesting book by Goodhardt, Ehrenberg, and Collins describes much of their early work,[8] with their later work covered by a collection authored by Barwise and Ehrenberg.[1] This school of research has produced many findings, most of which do not strictly pertain to the contents of this chapter, but merit mention in this book nevertheless.

Ratings Models

The networks have sunk substantial sums into research on estimating ratings, for the most part without success. Since 1980, however, academic journals have recorded advances in this area.

Gensch and Shaman introduced a model which accurately estimates the total number of viewers of network television at any particular time.[6,7] These numbers may be used as a baseline on which to build models which predict the ratings of individual programs. Their model uses a trigonometric time series approach, and models seasonality in television viewing.

Horen developed a model to estimate the ratings of individual programs.[11] His model uses past ratings data and other program attributes to predict future program ratings. He then uses the predicted ratings in a program scheduling model, which is reviewed in the next section. Horen's regression-like approach does not model audience flow, except for the inclusion of a "lead-in" variable, and does not consider viewing choice at the individual level or even segment level.

The Rust–Alpert Model

The Rust–Alpert model may be extended to provide ratings predictions which overcome the shortcomings of the Horen approach. Ratings may be predicted one time period in advance (as would be appropriate for evaluating a proposed schedule change), for an entire day (as would be appropriate for evaluating a new fall schedule), or for anything in between.

The Rust–Alpert viewing choice model uses flow state, program type, and audience segmentation to estimate the utilities of viewing options in particular viewer situations. Another variable that seems likely to affect utility is program quality. In the case of movies, quality (as measured by box office performance) has been successfully related to viewing.[14] The variable was omitted in the Rust–Alpert model only because there were insufficient data to permit its estimation.

The word *quality* is used here only as convenience. More accurately, we might speak of *segment-specific utility* or some other name which would imply that what we are really talking about is that which induces a viewer to watch, rather than some measure of esthetics or the skill of technical production.

To make this variable's use more specific, let the program-segment combination be the particular combination that corresponds to individual i and viewing option v. If there are n_j segments and n_p programs, then there are $(n_j \cdot n_p)$ such combinations. We define a vector **Q** of length $[(n_j \cdot n_p) - 1]$ which contains dummy variables indicating which combination is occurring. We may then obtain the following:

$$u(i, v) = \mu + \mathbf{B}_1\mathbf{F} + \mathbf{B}_2\mathbf{T} + \mathbf{B}_3\mathbf{Q} + e_{iv} \qquad (6.3)$$

where $\mathbf{B}_3$ is a coefficient vector whose elements may be interpreted as relative perceived quality.

Estimates for the quality coefficients may first be gained residually. In fact, even in its current form, the Rust–Alpert model has the attractive feature of allowing relative quality to be inferred by the degree of overestimation or underestimation of audience shares. Eventually, historical quality estimates for established programs may then be used to more accurately estimate succeeding years' ratings. Quality estimates for new programs should probably take into account both historical data and judgment. In this case, historical data would indicate past quality performance of previous new programs of that program type. Judgment could be added from the prescreening of pilot episodes, something that is already routinely done by advertising agencies.

Once the quality variable is added to the model, the potential accuracy of ratings predictions is enhanced. Estimates of total viewing at a particular time may be obtained from an aggregate model,[6,7] and these estimates may then be combined with the share estimates provided by the extended Rust–Alpert model.

Given aggregate data about the proportion of a segment which is continuing to watch or starting to watch, the model provides estimates for the probability that an individual in a particular flow state and segment will watch viewing option v^*. The estimated share of viewing option v^* within segment j is thus:

$$s(v^*,j) = \left[\sum c(i,v^*)\right] / \, nseg \qquad (6.4)$$

where *nseg* is the number of people in segment j, and the summation is over all of the people in segment j.

For a large population, this is equivalent to

$$s(v^*,j) = \sum [y(x,j) \cdot c_j(i,v^*; x)] \qquad (6.5)$$

where x is a variable indicating which program was watched in the preceding time period or whether the set was off; $y(x,j)$ is the proportion of segment j that viewed x in the previous time period; $c_j(i,v^*; x)$ is the estimated proportion of segment j which would view v^*, given that it had just engaged in viewing choice x; and the summation is over the prior viewing choices x.

Then if t^* is the time at which v^* is shown, $w(j,t^*)$ is the relative aggregate share of audience of segment j at time t^*, $A(t^*)$ is the total audience at time t^*, and $R(v^*)$ is the estimated rating (in proportions) for v^*, we have

$$R(v^*) = A(t^*) \cdot \sum [w(j,t^*) \cdot s(v^*,j)] \qquad (6.6)$$

These would be computed in a "simulation" in which ratings of earlier time periods would be estimated first, and those estimated ratings would in turn be input to the ratings estimations of later time periods. This "simulated" rating estimation procedure would be of use in estimating ratings for new seasons and schedule changes. For example, while deciding how much to spend for programs in a new fall network television schedule, an advertising agency may wish to simulate audience response to the schedule. Without simulating audience flow, judgmental rating estimation methods may fail to properly incorporate lead-in and bridging effects.

A network contemplating a midseason schedule change may also wish to simulate the consequences beforehand. Estimating reaction to an altered program schedule is also very important to advertising agencies.

Another benefit of including a quality variable in the utility model is that the quality of a program to a segment may be tracked over time. If there is a clear trend of increasing or decreasing quality, then extrapolating this trend may provide a better measure of the program's future potential than past ratings performance (which may be confounded by the quality of competiton and other factors).

The Henry–Rinne Model

Henry and Rinne[10] developed a model similar in concept to two of its predecessors, the Rust–Alpert model, and the Horen model described in the next section. They used a regression approach to estimate choice, using a logit dependent variable.

The guts of their model can be written as

$$y = \mathbf{A}(\mathbf{Xa} + \mathbf{E}) \qquad (6.7)$$

where $y = \ln(p_1/p.)$; p_1 is the proportional rating of vehicle i; p is the geometric mean of the proportional ratings in the time slot; **A** is a constant matrix; **X** is a matrix containing information about the vehicles; **a** is a coefficient vector; and **E** is an error vector.

Their model formulation requires considerable information, including preference. It incorporates audience flow only to the extent of inclusion of variables for "lead-in" and "lead-out," which takes into account the prior ratings of the programs before and after the modeled time slot.

Program Scheduling Models

Given that it is possible to accurately predict ratings, a useful application of program scheduling models to a television station or network is that of determining the optimal program schedule. A typical criterion of optimality would be profit maximization, but other criteria, such as ratings maximization, might also be used.

Horen made the first sophisticated attempt in this area.[11] Given the ratings prediction method described previously, he used an integer programming formulation to maximize a network's expected ratings. Due to the computational complexity, a search routine was used to find an approximate solution to the linear program.

Horen's method pioneered work in this area, but had some important limitations. His model did not consider audience segmentation, which resulted in such curious "optimal" scheduling as the family-oriented "Waltons" at ten o'clock at night. As was discussed previously, the ratings estimation component of the model (intentionally simplified to maintain linearity) also failed to adequately capture audience flow.

Henry and Rinne attacked a similar problem.[9] They conducted simulations to determine the best general strategies for a network. For example, is it better to compete head-on-head with the competitors' best programs, or to avoid scheduling the best programs in tough time slots? They stopped short of selection of an optimal schedule.

Current research by Rust, Eechambadi, and Alpert involves optimal scheduling using the Rust–Alpert viewing choice model. Profit is maximized, operationalized as the weighted sum of the ratings across the relevant audience segments. That is, each segment is weighted by its estimated commercial potential. In other words, a time slot in which a desirable viewer segment is well represented will likely command more money, and the total estimate is captured by the weighted sum.

The R–E–A approach uses a two-step assignment process. First the program is assigned to a day; then the programs within a day are optimally ordered. The ordering of the programs within a day is accomplished using complete enumeration of the possibilities. This is feasible because the number of programs in a day is reasonably small.

Assignment of programs to days, however, involves a vast number of possible combinations, which necessitates a search routine. A novel approach called a *stochastic gradient procedure* is being used for this purpose. Complete description of the procedure would involve too much technical detail for our purposes. Let it suffice to say that the optimization uses elements of

Monte Carlo simulation in the assignment of programs to days, for the purpose of avoiding as many local optima as possible.

Surprisingly, preliminary results indicate the potential of even the last-place network to make radical ratings improvements (sometimes in the range of 20–30 percent) by ordering the schedule properly.

References

1. T.P. Barwise and A.S.C. Ehrenberg, *Television and Its Audience: Recent Research at the LBS* (London: London Business School, May 1984).

2. Robert Bower, *Television and the Public* (New York: Holt, Rinehart and Winston, 1973).

3. Rene Y. Darmon, "Determinants of TV Viewing," *Journal of Advertising Research* (December 1976):17–24.

4. Ronald E. Frank and Marshall G. Greenberg, "Interest Based Segments of TV Audiences," *Journal of Advertising Research* (October 1979):43–52.

5. Ronald E. Frank and Marshall G. Greenberg, *The Public's Use of Television* (Beverly Hills: Sage, 1980).

6. Dennis H. Gensch and Paul Shaman, "Models of Competitive Television Ratings," *Journal of Marketing Research* (August 1980):307–15.

7. Dennis H. Gensch and Paul Shaman, "Predicting TV Ratings," *Journal of Advertising Research* (August 1980):85–92.

8. G.J. Goodhardt, A.S.C. Ehrenberg, and M.A. Collins, *The Television Audience: Patterns of Viewing* (Lexington, Mass.: Lexington Books, 1975).

9. Michael D. Henry and Heikki J. Rinne, "Offensive versus Defensive TV Programming Strategies," *Journal of Advertising Research* (June–July 1984):45–46.

10. Michael D. Henry and Heikki J. Rinne, "Predicting Program Shares in New Time Slots," *Journal of Advertising Research* (April/May 1984):9–17.

11. Jeffrey H. Horen, "Scheduling of Network Television Programs," *Management Science* (April 1980):354–70.

12. Fred N. Kerlinger and Elazur J. Pedhazur, *Multiple Regression in Behavioral Research* (New York: Holt, Rinehart and Winston, 1973).

13. Donald R. Lehmann, "Television Show Preference: Application of a Choice Model," *Journal of Marketing Research* (February 1971):47–55.

14. Barry R. Litman, "Predicting TV Ratings for Theatrical Movies," *Journalism Quarterly* (1979):590–94.

15. R. Duncan Luce, "The Choice Axiom after Twenty Years," *Journal of Mathematical Psychology* (1977):215–33.

16. R. Duncan Luce, *Individual Choice Behavior: A Theoretical Analysis* (New York: John Wiley & Sons, 1959).

17. Roland T. Rust and Mark I. Alpert, "An Audience Flow Model of Television Viewing Choice," *Marketing Science* (Spring 1984):113–124.

18. Kathryn E.A. Villani, "Personality/Life Style and Television Viewing Behavior," *Journal of Marketing Research* (November 1975):432–39.

19. Fred S. Zufryden, "Media Scheduling: A Stochastic Dynamic Model Approach," *Management Science* (August 1973):1395–1406.

Appendix 6A: An Audience Flow Model of Television Viewing Choice

Roland T. Rust
Mark I. Alpert

In 1981, an estimated $10 billion were spent by television advertisers (*Advertising Age* 1982). With advertising production costs and other costs figured in, the total investment in television advertising was even larger than that. Since viewing choice has a substantial impact on the ability to attract and effectively allocate these dollars, it is very important to both the advertisers and the television industry that television viewing choice be better understood. In addition, the many new choices made possible by the proliferation of cable and other new video technology make such an understanding of viewing choice especially timely.

Viewing choice may be described at either the aggregate level or the individual level. Recent advances in aggregate ratings estimation have been proposed by Horen (1980) and Gensch and Shaman (1980a, b). Horen's model uses past ratings data and other program attributes to predict future program ratings. The ratings model is then used as a basis for choosing optimal program scheduling from the network's perspective.

The Gensch and Shaman model uses a trigonometric time series approach to estimate the aggregate television audience at different days, hours, and seasons. An important conclusion from the accuracy of their model is that the aggregate television audience is highly predictable, and does not appear to be much affected by which programs are being shown.

One may infer from this empirical generalization that the viewing choice process may be usefully considered as a two-stage process. In stage one, the individual chooses whether or not to watch, and in stage two determines

---

Reprinted by permission, "An Audience Flow Model of Television Viewing Choice," Roland T. Rust and Mark I. Alpert, *Marketing Science,* Vol. 3, No. 2, Spring 1984.

The authors thank Simmons Market Research Bureau, Inc. for supplying the data used in the analysis. The helpful comments of Donald G. Morrison, Subrata K Sen, an anonymous section editor, and two anonymous reviewers are much appreciated.

which program to view. The Gensch and Shaman results imply that the first stage can be effectively predicted, and that the two stages may be modeled independently. This appendix proposes a method of modeling the second stage of the viewing choice process.

To model this choice stage of television viewing, however, it is necessary to describe behavior at the individual level. Many aggregate exposure models have been proposed which acknowledge different exposure probabilities for each individual (for example, Greene and Stock 1967; Chandon 1976; Rust and Klompmaker 1981). Evidence that these exposure probabilities are nonstationary (Schreiber 1974) has led to nonstationary exposure models (Sabavala and Morrison 1981). All of these models clearly reflect the fact that individual differences occur in viewing choice. Much less is known, however, about why these differences occur.

Consideration of past research in viewing choice suggests a useful conceptual framework for building an individual viewing choice model. The proposed model integrates the concepts of utility, audience flow, and audience segmentation.

Lehmann (1971) developed a utility model which used variables related to program type and quality of production to predict the preference of television shows. The model did not predict viewing behavior as such, but suggested profitable directions for the development of viewing choice utility models.

Viewing choice involves more than just preference, because the channel to which a television set is currently tuned will tend to remain on, unless effort is expended to change the channel. For purposes of consistency, this appendix will refer to these effects of channel inertia and lead-in as "audience flow" effects.

Horen (1980) made a partial allowance for these effects by including a lead-in variable in his aggregate model. Other current research explores the use of Markov chains to model audience flow phenomena (Zackon 1981). It is possible to integrate conceptually audience flow effects into a utility framework, if it is assumed that the effort expenditure required to change channels involves some disutility.

The viewing behavior of audience segments has been another fertile area of research (Bower 1973; Gensch and Ranganathan 1974; Villani 1975; Goodhardt *et al.* 1975; Frank and Greenberg 1979, 1980). Consistent with the spirit of this past research, the proposed model assumes that individuals within a viewing segment possess similar viewing option utilities, given that audience flow effects are held constant.

The purpose of this appendix is to develop and test a model of individual viewing choice. The model incorporates utility, audience flow, and audience segmentation, and is tested on large-sample network television data.

§1 presents the assumptions and formulation of the model, and §2 discusses the model's estimation. §3 describes the data, the results of estimating the model, and the results of a large sample cross-validated predictive test. §4 includes conclusions, an illustration of the model's use, and a discussion of the managerial implications and limitations of the model.

1. Model Description

Assumptions

Let us denote the utility of viewing half-hour program segment (viewing option) v to individual i as $u(i,v)$, with corresponding probability of choice $c(i,v)$. Consistent with the Luce axiom (Luce 1959, 1977), we assume that the probability of individual i viewing half-hour program segment v^*, given that he or she has chosen to watch television that half hour, is:

$$c(i,v^*) = u(i,v^*) / \sum_{v \in S} u(i,v) \tag{6A–1}$$

where S is the time slot corresponding to v^*.

The model segments the population by age, education, and sex. With these divisions, there are eight (2 × 2 × 2) demographic segments (table 6A–1)—although other splits and segments could be explored if desired. For reasons of parsimony and ease of estimation, the viewing segments are assumed to be homogeneous in the construction of utilities. Thus, two individuals from the same segment, other factors being equal, would be assumed to have the same choice probabilities.[1]

Programs are assumed to be classifiable into one of nine program types: serial drama, action drama, psychological drama, game show, talk, variety, movie, news, and sports or comedy. These program types are similar to ones

Table 6A–1
Description of Segments

Segment	*Description*		*Count*	*Sum of Weights*	*Abbreviation*
1 older (≥ 35)	uneducated (≤ 11 yrs)	women	170	564.4	(OUW)
2 older	educated	women	938	2,420.0	(OEW)
3 younger	uneducated	women	574	1,968.8	(YUW)
4 younger	educated	women	1,357	2,727.6	(YEW)
5 older	uneducated	men	81	426.1	(OUM)
6 older	educated	men	780	2,410.2	(OEM)
7 younger	uneducated	men	371	1,691.8	(YUM)
8 younger	educated	men	1,163	2,256.2	(YEM)

Table 6A–2
Description of Flow States

Flow State	*Description*			F_1	F_2	F_3	F_4	F_5
1	set on	right channel	start	1	0	0	0	0
2	set on	right channel	continuation	0	1	0	0	0
3	set on	wrong channel	start	0	0	1	0	0
4	set on	wrong channel	continuation	0	0	0	1	0
5	set off		start	0	0	0	0	1
6	set off		continuation	−1	−1	−1	−1	−1

found by factor analysis[2] (Gensch and Ranganathan 1974) and have previously been used to significantly improve the estimation of television audience duplication (Headen, Klompmaker, and Rust 1979). Utilities derived from the particular program types are allowed to vary across the segments. The model assumes that different program types may have different utility to different segments. Hence a distinct set of program type utilities is estimated for each segment.

There are assumed to be six "flow states" which may affect the utility of a viewing option (see table 6A–2). A separate flow state exists for each combination of individual and viewing option in a particular half-hour period. The flow state incorporates information as to whether the television was off or on already; if the set was on, whether it was tuned to the same channel on which the viewing option is appearing; and whether or not the viewing option is the continuation of a program already in progress. To reduce computational requirements, the utilities derived from these flow states are assumed for this demonstration to be constant across the segments.

As an example of how a flow state may be expected to affect utility, consider the fourth flow state (see table 6A–2). The set is already on, and it is tuned to a channel different from that on which the viewing represents the continuation of a program. It would seem reasonable to expect the utility of this flow state to be low.

Summarizing, the model assumes that the probability of choice corresponding to an individual and viewing option is predictable using the individual's demographic segment, the program type of the viewing option, and the flow state corresponding to the individual and viewing option.

Formulation

The utility of viewing option v to individul i may be seen as a mean utility plus a deviation from the mean. In other words, variables relating to the viewing option and the individual may be used to explain why a particular program has more utility than average or less utility than average to an individual at a particular time. The model specifies explanatory variables to explain these deviations. The model is formulated as a regression model with effect coded variables (Kerlinger and Pedhazur 1973). Effect coding is a variation of dummy variable coding which allows interpretations similar to that of analysis of variance.

The flow state variable **F** (see table 6A–2) is a vector corresponding to viewing option v and individual i, which reflects whether the television was previously on or off; if it was on, whether it was tuned to the same channel as v; and whether v is the start or continuation of a program. For example, if the set has just been turned on, and viewing option v is the start of a program, then flow state 5 applies. The fifth element of **F** would be 1 and the other elements would be 0. Since the vector is used to determine utility deviations from the mean, the sixth and last flow state would be coded as -1 for each of the five elements of **F**.

The program type variable **T** is a vector corresponding to viewing option v and individual i, which reflects the segment of individual i and the program type of viewing option v. If there are n_s segments and n_t program types, then **T** is of length $(n_s \cdot n_t) - 1$. The vector **T**, like **F**, is effect coded. Thus, the intersection of segment n_s and program type n_t would result in -1 for all of the elements of **T**. Otherwise, the intersection of segment s and program type t would result in elements $n_s(t - 1) + s$ of **T** being equal to 1, while the rest would be 0.

Using the variables defined above, it is possible to express concisely the utility of viewing option v to individual i:

$$u(i,v) = \bar{u} + \mathbf{B}_1\mathbf{F} + \mathbf{B}_2\mathbf{T} + \epsilon_{iv} \qquad (6A\text{–}2)$$

where $\bar{u}$ is the overall mean utility across the groups defined by variables **F** and **T**, where **F** and **T** are defined as above, ϵ_{iv} represents the unexplained deviation (assumed to be normally distributed), and $\mathbf{B}_1$ and $\mathbf{B}_2$ are coefficient vectors.

2. Estimation

Each individual in the television sample used here (Simmons 1978a) has a sampling weight, which is inversely proportional to that individual's probability of selection. To produce estimates for the population using the above model, it is necessary to incorporate these weights into the analysis. The resulting appropriate statistical methodology is weighted least squares regression with effect vectors, where the weights are the sampling weights.

This effect coded regression is formally identical to analysis of variance. The regression formulation is used to handle more easily the computational complications caused by the weighted observations and the fact that the analysis of variance would involve a difficult unbalanced incomplete block design.

Also, regression using effect coded variables has several desirable properties (summarized from Kerlinger and Pedhazur 1973):

1. Each element of the coefficient vector represents a deviation from the overall mean.
2. Similar to analysis of variance, a predicted score is the sum of the overall mean and the appropriate coefficient vector elements.
3. The analysis of data with unequal cell sizes (such as appear in this appendix) proceeds in the same manner as that for equal cell sizes.

The coefficient vector elements may be usefully interpreted as utility deviations. For example, the first element of $\mathbf{B}_2$ reflects the deviation from mean utility attributable to program type 1 for segment 1. If the first program type is relatively unappealing to segment 1, for example, the respective element of $\mathbf{B}_2$ would be negative.

In order to use the model predictively, it is first necessary to estimate the coefficients of the model. The dependent variable, $u(i,v^*)$, is not observable. Thus, it is necessary to approximate $u(i,v^*)$, using (6A–1), which may be reexpressed as:

$$\hat{u}(i,v^*) = c(i,v^*) \sum_{v \in S} u(i,v). \tag{6A–3}$$

The quantity $\Sigma_{v \in S} u(i,v)$ may be considered a measure of the relative attractiveness or strength of v's time slot. If the quantity is large, then the implication may be that two or three high-utility programs are being shown then. A viewing option may have high utility, but still have a mediocre probability of being viewed if it is competing against other high-utility options. Conversely, even a low-utility program might fare reasonably well in a weak time slot.

Thus, if information were known on the strength of the time slots, the viewing choices could be more reliably used to estimate utility. If the (temporary) assumption is made that the time slots are of equal strength, and the arbitrary value of 1 is chosen as the sum of the utilities in each time slot, then we have:

$$\hat{u}(i,v^*) = c(i,v) \cdot 1 = c(i,v). \tag{6A–4}$$

Since large-sample estimates of $c(i,v)$ may be obtained directly from panel data, the assumption of equal strengths for the time slots implies that regression may be employed to estimate the coefficients of the model.

However, once the coefficients are estimated, they may be used to reestimate the utility of each viewing option:

$$\hat{\hat{u}}(i,v^*) = \bar{u} + \mathbf{B_1F} + \mathbf{B_2T}. \qquad (6A\text{–}5)$$

Then using the above reestimated utilities, the relative strength $k(S)$ of each time slot S may be reestimated:

$$\hat{k}(S) = \sum_{v \in S} \hat{\hat{u}}(i,v). \qquad (6A\text{–}6)$$

The relative strengths of the time slots enable the reestimation of each viewing option's utility:

$$\hat{u}(i,v^*) = \hat{k}(S) \cdot c(i,v^*). \qquad (6A\text{–}7)$$

The new estimates may then be used as the dependent variable values for a new regression. The new coefficient estimates then obtained should be better, since the revised dependent variable takes into consideration improved estimates of the relative strengths of the time slots. This procedure is repeated until the coefficient values converge. A flow chart of the iterative procedure is presented in figure 6A–1.

In the first iteration the dependent variable is the audience share (in proportions) for the viewing options in a particular time slot for a particular combination of segment and prior program (or none). The prior program (or none), combined with a current viewing option, defines the flow state variable **F** (table 6A–2). The segment, combined with the program type of a viewing option, defines the program type variable **T**. The unit of analysis is the intersection of segment and prior program (or none). For each unit, there is a separate data point corresponding to each viewing option. In this estimation, 895 data points result from the combinations of time slot, prior program, and viewing option, with each data point comprised of many individuals who share the independent variable values.

The estimation performed at each step of the iterative procedure is mathematically equivalent to using the individual as the unit of analysis. It is for computational convenience that individuals are aggregated by segment and prior program (or none) viewed. A weighted least squares regression is performed, in which the weight for a particular segment and prior program combination is the sum of the sampling weights for the individuals in that segment who viewed that particular prior program.

The coefficients obtained using this method of aggregation are identical to those that would be obtained without aggregating, but the R^2 is necessarily higher (Kmenta 1971, pp. 325–28). The R^2 from the aggregated analysis

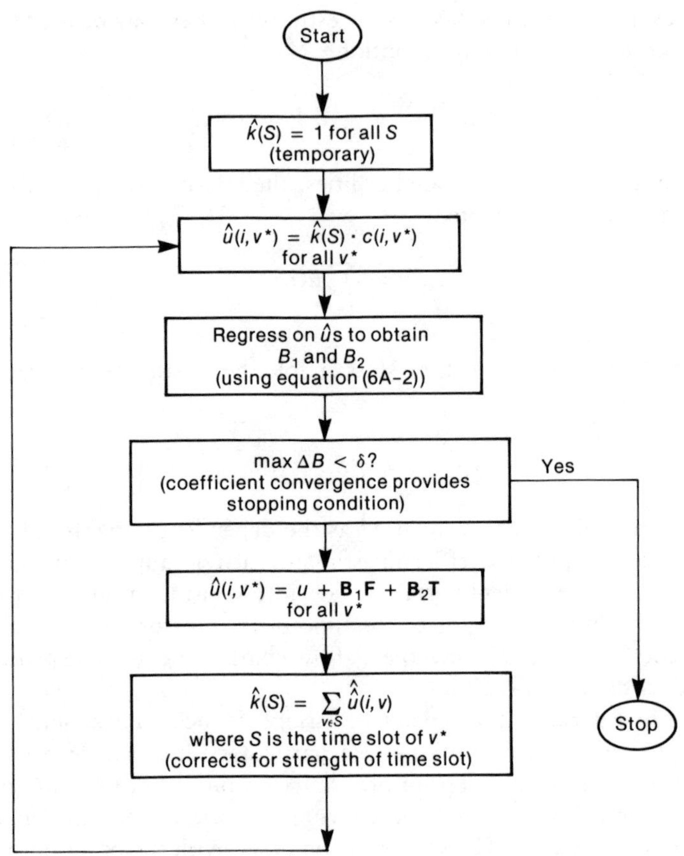

Figure 6A–1. Iterative Estimation Procedure

may provide a truer picture of the accuracy of the model (Morrison 1972; 1973). In any event the choice of reported R^2 does not affect the major findings of this appendix.

3. Empirical Analysis

Data

The data used to estimate and test the model were collected by Simmons (1978a, b). Their respondents were selected using a national multistage area cluster sample. Television viewing data were collected from 5,652 respondents in fall 1977, of which 5,434 were usable respondents for this analysis.

Table 6A–3
Regression Coefficients from Final Iteration

Flow State	*Coefficient B_1*
1	−0.094
2	0.814
3	−0.275
4	−0.310
5	0.036
6	−0.171 $(= -\Sigma B_1)$

Table 6A–4
Program Type Coefficients B_2

Segment	*Action Drama*	*Psychological Drama*	*Comedy*	*Sports*	*Movie*
1 (OUW)	−0.139	0.109	−0.019	−0.070	0.020
2 (OEW)	−0.130	0.080	−0.030	−0.018	0.046
3 (YUW)	−0.098	0.012	−0.018	−0.092	−0.070
4 (YEW)	−0.102	0.009	0.026	−0.029	0.011
5 (OUM)	−0.115	0.045	−0.043	0.157	−0.001
6 (OEM)	−0.074	−0.020	−0.073	0.148	−0.034
7 (YUM)	0.029	0.075	0.001	0.157	0.025
8 (YEM)	−0.075	−0.040	−0.041	0.244	0.137 $(= -\Sigma B_2)$

Estimation Results

The model coefficients were estimated using the prime-time program data for Monday and Thursday. There were 12 half-hour time slots, involving 34 viewing options[3] and 18,522 individual viewing choices.

The iterative procedure converged after eight iterations, yielding the final coefficient values reported in table 6A–4. In the first iteration, in which viewing share was the dependent variable, an adjusted R^2 of 0.85 was obtained. Thus the model provides good explanation of viewing choice, even without iteratively adjusting for the relative strength of the time periods.

Subsequent iterations progressively refined the dependent variable to more closely correspond to utility, using equation (6A–3). By the eighth iteration the adjusted R^2 had risen to 0.93. Because an iterative procedure is employed, and the dependent variable is not directly observable, many of the usual interpretations of R^2 may not be made. Nevertheless, the high R^2, coupled with the trend of the fit accuracy increasing over the iterations, is a reassuring check of the internal consistency of the model.

Because the iterative nature of the analysis may produce dependencies, the usual hypothesis tests on the variables may not strictly be performed. The model's accuracy must be assessed on the basis of its accuracy of prediction in a large sample cross-validation, as seen in the next section.

However, some insight may be gained if one assumes that the dependent variable in the final iteration is an independent and valid measure of utility. This assumption may not be too bad, considering the rise in R^2 over the iterations, and the intuitive justification for the dependent variable adjustment in the iterative procedure.

Given this assumption, the significance of the variables may be tested using nested F tests of the incremental gains in explained variance (Namboodiri *et al.* 1975) Using degrees of freedom adjusted to reflect the weighted nature of the analysis, both the flow state variable **F** and the program type variable **T** are found to be significant at the 0.01 level.

Further (face) validity checks are provided by an examination of the signs and magnitudes of the flow state coefficients. All are as would be anticipated. For example, the second flow state has a large positive coefficient. This flow state corresponds to a situation in which the set is already on and tuned to the right channel, and while the viewing option represents the continuation of a program; for example, someone is in the middle of watching a program. It seems reasonable to associate a relatively high utility with the program's continuation.

Examination of the program type coefficients provides a further validity check. Once again, they appear to be quite reasonable. For example, the highest utility increment is associated with the intersection of the eighth segment (young educated men) and sports programming. The advertising profession has long known that sports programming is attractive to this economically important market segment. The week-end time slots when large numbers of young educated men are watching have long been used by networks for sports programming. It is also interesting that all of the female segments have a negative utility deviation associated with sports.

Prediction Results

The model's ability to predict individual viewing choice was tested using prime-time programs on Wednesday and Friday. These days were chosen in an attempt to pick typical days of the week while minimizing overlap with the programs used to estimate the model. Different weeks were used, to further maximize the difference between the estimation programs and the validation programs. There were 12 half-hour time slots used in the validation, involving 30 viewing options[4] and 19,050 individual viewing choices.

At every time slot, the viewing choice made by each individual was compared to the choice predicted by the model, based on the individual's segment

Table 6A–5
Predictive Accuracy of Four Viewing Models

Model	*Description*	*Proportion of Correct Prediction*
1	Proposed model	0.762
2	"Random choice"	0.406
3	"Watch until program conclusion"	0.646
4	"Stay with a program type"	0.591

and flow states (taking into account the individual's viewing choice the previous half hour), and the program types of the program alternatives.

Three simple models were also tested. The first model assumes random program choice. The second model assumes that an individual will choose randomly except that when he or she starts a program, he or she will watch it to the end. The third model assumes that an individual will first choose randomly, but then will stick with that program type, if possible. The predictive results of these four models are shown in table 6A–5. *Z* tests of the differences between the prediction proportions show that the proposed model predicted significantly better than each of the three simpler models at beyond the 0.01 level. The proposed model predicted viewing choice correctly 76 percent of the time (corresponding to a mean prediction error of two rating points), whereas the accuracy of the simpler models ranged from 41 percent to 65 percent. (See table 6A–5.)

Conclusion, Implications, and Limitations

The proposed model is a successful predictor of individual viewing choice. Its 76-percent prediction accuracy represents a promising step in the effort to better understand this complex subject, an area marked by considerable economic importance and a paucity of previous empirical work. The empirical findings provide a baseline against which future models of individual viewing choice may be compared.

The theoretical framework also provides a foundation upon which other researchers in this area may build. The "audience flow" effects of lead-in and inertia of channel selection have been shown to improve prediction, as has the differential attraction of program types to the demographic segments of the viewers. While knowledge of these effects is not new, the proposed model provides a way of making these variables quantifiable and explicitly useful for explanation and prediction of individual viewing choice.

To exemplify the potential managerial usefulness of the proposed model to television networks and advertising agencies, let us consider the evaluation of the impact on audience of a proposed schedule change. We assume that the existing program will be (or might be) replaced by an alternate program whose program type is known.

The researcher evaluating this programming shift using the proposed model would perform the following steps:

1. Estimate seasonally-adjusted aggregate audiences for each network and time slot, by segment. Existing models (Gensch and Shaman 1980a, b) have been shown to produce accurate estimates.
2. Estimate the proportions turning the television on or off which produce the incremental changes in aggregate audience. These proportions may be approximated using historical Nielsen or Simmons data.
3. From steps 1 and 2, the number of viewers of the time slot in which the schedule change is planned has been approximated for each combination of segment and prior program (or none) watched. Equation (6A–1) may now be used to estimate, for each combination of segment and prior program, the proportion that will view each of the programs in the revised time slot.
4. Step 3 may be successively repeated for subsequent time periods to provide an idea of the effects of the switch on later time periods. The model implies that the *later* time periods' audiences will be affected by an earlier program change, due to the lead-in aspect of the flow state variable.
5. If the network is evaluating the programming shift, it may examine the results of several different program types, choosing to substitute a program type that will both result in a high rating for that half hour and provide an effective lead-in to the network's subsequent programs.

Table 6A–6 presents an illustration of the results of applying this procedure to predicting audience proportions for a possible change in the program schedule for a given time slot. Applying the model using the estimated proportions of each segment watching television during this time slot, as well as the coefficients from the estimation sample, produced the predicted audience for the NBC show "Grizzly Adams" and its competitors. One may note that the predicted audiences were close to those actually observed.[5] Predicted versus actual audiences broken down by demographic segment are shown for the NBC show. (The others are omitted for brevity.)

Schedule changes are evaluated for two proposed revisions, both of which result in higher predicted ratings for NBC. Replacing "Grizzly Adams" with a psychological drama would be predicted to increase the audience from 0.08 to 0.10, and replacement by a sports program would result in even more of an increase (to 0.11). Which of these moves might be preferred by NBC would depend not only on costs and expected aggregate ratings, but also the

Table 6A–6
Estimated Audiences for Example Program Substitutions

	Segment	Current		Revised	
		("Grizzly Adams")		*(Psych. Drama)*	*(Sports)*
		Predicted	*Actual*	*Predicted*	*Predicted*
NBC Segment Audiences	1 (OUW)	0.09	0.10	0.14	0.10
Proportion of Segment in NBC Viewing Audience	2 (OEW)	0.07	0.10	0.11	0.09
	3 (YUW)	0.09	0.07	0.12	0.10
	4 (YEW)	0.08	0.05	0.09	0.09
	5 (OUM)	0.09	0.11	0.13	0.15
	6 (OEM)	0.08	0.10	0.09	0.11
	7 (YUM)	0.07	0.09	0.08	0.09
	8 (YEM)	0.07	0.05	0.08	0.11
Aggregate Audiences	*Network*				
Proportion of Total Viewing Audiences	NBC	0.08	0.08	0.10	0.11
	ABC ("Eight is Enough")	0.10	0.12	0.11	0.10
	CBS ("Good Times")	0.10	0.08	0.07	0.07

expected appeal of each replacement to the audience segments of interest to NBC's advertisers. One could weight the proportions of each segment by the number estimated as viewing at this time, to determine not only the aggregate audience ratings, but also the audience composition delivered to advertisers. In this case, advertisers seeking male target markets may prefer the sports program, while females may be better reached with the psychological drama. These changes in the segment audiences also affect the lead-in to subsequent time slots.

As an extension to the proposed model, the relative attractiveness of programs might be used to revise the audience estimates. One preliminary method of doing this might be to use the residuals from equation (6A–2). An unusually attractive program within a program type would be expected to have a large positive residual.

Some limitations of the model should be noted. The model is tested on network viewing data. It is conceivable that an empirical test including cable programs and local programs may have been less successful. Nevertheless, the model may easily be applied to these expanded alternative sets, and expanded if necessary to include variables specific to the inclusion of cable and/or local programs.

Very popular programs will tend to have underestimated choice probabilities, since programs within a program type are assumed to have equal utility to a given segment. This problem may be remedied for returning programs by including a program-specific variable based upon historical data.

The model does not explain why individuals turn the television on. This is an important issue for further research. Also, all of the traditional limitations of diary data qualify the validity of the empirical results, as does the fact that the data used may not necessarily be representative of data gathered from other days, seasons, or years.

The proposed model provides an explicit model basis for future research in television viewing choice, and suggests a systematic method for considering the comparative impact on both immediate and subsequent audience size and composition of alternative programs within specified time slots.

Notes

1. Some confidence in the validity of the assumption of demographic segment homogeneity in choice probabilities may be drawn from the results of variations in program choices between versus within segments. Multivariate analysis of variance found significant variations among segments in terms of the relative probabilities of individuals within segments viewing the nine program types (Wilks's Lambda = 0.71, significant at beyond 0.001). Hence, the variation between segments was significantly greater than the variation within segments in choice behavior. Inspection of relative frequencies of program viewing across segments shows a generally expected pattern of viewing behavior (for example, "sports programs far more likely to be viewed by males than by females of all education levels," and so forth).

2. The factor analysis approach to defining program types has not been without controversy. While Kirsch and Banks (1962), Wells (1969), and Frank, Becknell, and Clokey (1971) arrived at results similar to those of Gensch and Ranganathan, Ehrenberg (1968) was unable to discover the meaningful program types using factor analysis.

3. The programs in the estimation sample included 6 action dramas, 10 psychological dramas, 5 movies, 8 comedies, and 5 sports programs. Since the programs were chosen from prime time, it is not surprising that no serial dramas or game shows (normally shown in the morning), variety/talk shows (normally shown in the late evening), or news shows (normally shown in the early or late evening) were encountered in the estimation sample.

4. The validation sample consists of 12 action dramas, 2 psychological dramas, 10 movies, and 6 comedies.

5. The aggregate audiences do not sum to one because there are nonviewers in the population. Also the numbers reported here are somewhat lower than those typically encountered in Nielsen audimeter data, due to the fact that they were tabulated from viewing diaries.

References

Advertising Age (1981). (February 16):S-4.

Bower, Robert (1973). *Television and Public.* New York: Holt, Rinehart and Winston.

Chandon, J.L.J. (1976). "A Comparative Study of Media Exposure Models," unpublished Ph.D. dissertation, Northwestern University, Evanston, Ill.

Ehrenberg, A.S.C. (1968). "The Factor Analytic Search for Program Types," *Journal of Advertising Research* 8:55–63.

Frank, Ronald E., James C. Becknell, and James D. Clokey (1971). "Television Program Types," *Journal of Marketing Research* 8 (May):204–11.

——— and Marshall G. Greenberg (1979). "Interest Based Segments of TV Audiences," *Journal of Advertising Research* 19 (October):43–52.

——— and ——— (1980). *The Public's Use of Television.* Beverly Hills: Sage.

Gensch, Dennis and B. Ranganathan (1974). "Evaluation of Television Program Content for the Purpose of Promotional Segmentation." *Journal of Marketing Research* 11 (November):390–98.

——— and Paul Shaman (1980a). "Predicting TV Ratings," *Journal of Advertising Research* 20 (August):85–92.

——— and ——— (1980b). "Models of Competitive Television Ratings," *Journal of Marketing Research* 17 (August):307–15.

Goodhardt, G.J., A.S.C. Ehrenberg, and M.A. Collins (1975), *The Television Viewing Audience: Patterns of Viewing.* New York: Saxon House.

Greene, J.D. and J.S. Stock (1967). *Advertising Reach and Frequency in Magazines.* New York: Marketmath Inc. and Reader's Digest Association.

Headen, Robert S., Jay E. Klompmaker, and Roland T. Rust (1979). "The Duplication of Viewing Law and Television Media Schedule Evaluation," *Journal of Marketing Research* 16 (August):333–40.

Horen, Jeffrey H. (1980). "Scheduling of Network Television Programs," *Management Science* 26 (April):354–70.

Kerlinger, Fred N. and Elazur J. Pedhazur (1973). *Multiple Regression in Behavioral Research.* New York: Holt, Rinehart and Winston.

Kirsch, Arthur D. and Seymour Banks (1962). "Program Types Defined by Factor Analysis," *Journal of Advertising Research* 2:29–31.

Kmenta, Jan (1971). *Elements of Econometrics.* New York: Macmillan.

Lehmann, Donald R. (1971). "Television Show Preference: Application of a Choice Model," *Journal of Marketing Research* 8 (February):47–55.

Luce, R. Duncan (1959), *Individual Choice Behavior: A Theoretical Analysis.* New York: John Wiley & Sons.

——— (1977). "The Choice Axiom After Twenty Years," *Journal of Mathematical Psychology* 15:215–33.

Morrison, Donald G. (1972). "Upper Bounds for Correlations between Binary Outcomes and Probabilistic Predictions," *Journal of the American Statistical Association* 67 (March):68–70.

——— (1973). "Evaluating Market Segmentation Studies: The Properties of R^2," *Management Science* 19 (July):1213–21.

Namboodiri, N.K., L.F. Carter, and H.M. Blalock, Jr. (1975). *Applied Multivariate Analysis and Experimental Designs.* New York: McGraw-Hill.

Rust, Roland T. and Jay E. Klompmaker (1981). "Improving the Estimation Procedure for the Beta Binomial TV Exposure Model," *Journal of Marketing Research* 18 (November):442–48.

Sabavala, Darius J. and Donald G. Morrison (1981), "A Nonstationary Model of Binary Choice Applied to Media Exposure," *Management Science* 27 (June): 637–57.

Schreiber, Robert J. (1974), "Instability in Media Exposure Habits," *Journal of Advertising Research* 14 (April):13–17.

Simmons Media Studies (1978a). *Selective Markets and the Media Reaching Them.* New York: Simmons Media Studies.

——— (1978b). *Technical Guide: 1977/1978 Study of Selective Markets and the Media Reaching Them.* New York: Simmons Media Studies.

Villani, Kathryn, E.A. (1975). "Personality/Life Style and Television Viewing Behavior," *Journal of Marketing Research* 12 (November):432–39.

Wells, William D. (1969), "The Rise and Fall of Television Program Types," *Journal of Advertising Research* 9:21–27.

Zackon, Richard (1981), unpublished personal correspondence.

7 Future Directions in Media Models

It is always hazardous to forecast the future, but one relatively reliable method of developing predictions is to project the implications of current developments. *Megatrends* author John Naisbitt uses this method by tracking the amount of space given to topics in daily newspapers.[6]

From my readings it seems likely that media models will be greatly affected by three major areas of change. First, there will be fundamental changes in the media environment, mostly due to the creation of new media. Second, there will be significant advances in audience measurement. Finally, there will be a great increase in the computational ability of computers.

New Developments in the Media Environment

Rapid change marks the media environment, especially in the proliferation of delivery systems for television. Cable television, video cassette recorders, pay-per-view, and satellite television together are guaranteed to produce large changes in the media environment.

Cable Television (CATV)

Cable television began as a way for residents of isolated communities to receive television. The television signals were brought in by microwave (or later, satellite) and dispersed throughout the community by cable. This characterization of the cable television audience is no longer accurate. Cable networks such as MTV and ESPN have arisen, and superstations such as Ted Turner's WTBS have been made available to tens of millions.

Cable is now viewed as a means of obtaining a larger number of viewing alternatives, and penetration in cities is growing rapidly. For example, in Austin, Texas, cable penetration is over 50 percent in spite of the fact that all three major networks plus an independent station are available locally without cable. The local cable company cannot keep up with the demand for new cable subscriptions.

What is seen in Austin is occurring all over the country. Still, media models have not yet discovered this new environment. Existing media models cover network television or spot television. There are few, if any, attempts to cover cable.

Mark Alpert and this author are currently working on a Marketing Science Institute grant (funded by ABC, CBS and MSI) to extend the Rust–Alpert audience flow model to the cable environment. It should also be possible to replicate in the cable environment some of the previous work on audience exposure, which was tested only on network television. There is clearly much work to do, and it is not obvious that the network models will work, without major modifications, on the cable televisiòn environment.

Video Cassette Recorders (VCRs)

Advertisers are worried about VCRs both because of the potential of "zapping" (passing over commercials)[4] and because VCRs give the consumer the alternative of renting movies for a modest price, and watching the television commercial-free. There is also the complication that by taping a program on a VCR an individual may view the program whenever he or she wants, perhaps even several times, or not at all. This wreaks havoc with the Nielsen assumption that if the television is turned on and tuned to a particular program, that it is being watched.

It is not obvious how to measure the use of VCRs with the precision that has become customary for network television viewing. Maybe the VCR could be wired up to a device similar to the Nielson audimeter. This is a major measurement problem, and without VCR use data, media models cannot be calibrated.

Pay Per View (PPV)

Pay Per View is a premium service, not to be confused with the subscription service provided by networks like HBO and Cinemax. In HBO, for example, the customer pays a set monthly fee, and then receives the channel for an entire month. In pay per view, by contrast, a two-way cable hookup permits the cable subscriber to select programs *one at a time* for a fee of, say, ten dollars.

PPV has not really caught on yet, primarily due to the fact that few cable systems have two-way cable. That situation is changing, as municipal cable contracts often require two-way capability. Some experts expect PPV to obtain top events such as the Olympics and the Super Bowl in the next few years. That may not happen, because the public uproar would be deafening if a substantial portion of the country (those without two-way cable) were denied the possibility of watching the Super Bowl! Nevertheless, PPV seems likely to become more of a factor in the coming years, and media models will have to include it.

One way pay-TV may become prevalent is through forcing satellite dish owners to pay for broadcasts through the use of a descrambler.[9]

Satellite Television (STV)

STV is the direct reception of television broadcasts via home satellite dishes.[8] The media experts have pronounced STV dead with great regularity, but a drive through the countryside or the suburbs reveals countless satellite dishes in people's yards.

The development of STV is paralleling the development of cable. It first began in remote rural communities where neither broadcast nor cable was available. Before long, however, people began to realize that the satellite dish gave access to more programming choices than even a cable system could. As the price of dishes became affordable to the middle class, STV proliferated.

Satellite reception has some unique problems for network advertisers and cable channels. Satellites are used to send the raw network feed, which means many commercials are missing. Cable channels are received for free, although some channels such as HBO are now starting to scramble their signal, requiring rental of a decoder.

Some of these descramblers are now "addressable."[9] This means that individual descramblers may be provided the satellite signal. This may be the back door to pay-per-view television for a substantial minority of the viewing public.

Satellite reception presents new difficulties to media modelers. These difficulties have not yet been tackled.

New Developments in Audience Measurement

Again the major developments here are likely to occur in television. They involve the improvement of qualitative measures of exposure and audience measurement using two-way cable. Measurement problems with VCRs, Pay Per View, and satellite television exist, but it is not at all clear at this point how to deal with them. Nevertheless, the president of the Advertising Research Foundation, Michael Naples, believes that institution of a comprehensive, automatic, computerized audience measurement system is inevitable.[7]

Two-Way Cable

Communities already exist in which a sample population is hooked up to a two-way cable system which enables direct measurement of viewing choice (similar to the use of the Nielsen audimeter) and also yields purchase information, using ID cards with bar codes and optical scanner technology.[10] The television signal may also be split to provide true experiments of advertising effectiveness.

It is unlikely that such a system could ever be implemented nationwide, because of invasion of privacy problems and the extraneous variables of VCRs, satellites, and other types of equipment. But it might be feasible to expand these networks to a wide enough area that they would be reasonably representative of the overall population. If this is accomplished, then models that develop and analyze advertising experiments will be required.

People Meters

Audience measurement in television is changing radically. Traditionally advertisers in the United States have relied to a large extent on automatic data provided by Nielsen using the electronic audimeter. This device measures whether a television set is on, and to what channel it is tuned. It has been criticized for not measuring the viewing behavior of people, and it has been pointed out that often the television is on even when there is no one watching.

The British company AGB perceived the audimeter's shortcoming as a market opportunity, and announced a new ratings device called a "people meter." The people meter would have a button for each viewer in a household, thus producing individual data rather than the household data provided by Nielsen.[1]

Perceiving a strong threat, Nielsen responded with a people meter of its own,[2] but it is not clear at this juncture how the battle between these media heavyweights will resolve itself.[3] It is clear, however, that the quality and usefulness of viewing data has been seriously questioned, which may point to a "measurement technology race" between the leading audience measurement companies.

New Computer Technology

A revolution in the computing power of a computer chip may influence the kind of media models that can be built. Computer chips currently in experimental production may multiply by many times the computing power of computers. The result may be that methods previously discarded as being too costly computationally will be revived.

Simulation models stand to gain the most from this. Currently they simply take too long to run to be useful. That very well might change in the next fifteen years. We can also expect that even more models previously (or currently) relegated to mainframe computers will become feasible on PCs.

At a handful of leading universities, notably the University of Illinois and the University of Texas, students are routinely expected to use computerized media models on PCs. Kent Lancaster, with the help of materials developed by John Leckenby and Arnold Barban, has created a useful set of materials for this purpose.[5]

Conclusion

Technology is rapidly changing the media environment, measurement methods, and computers. The result is a great need for new media models which more clearly reflect the realities of an increasingly technological, information-rich world. If anything, the challenges to the builders of media models appear even greater than they did in the early days of computers, when the media environment and available data were much simpler.

References

1. Verne Gay, "Nielsen: Metering Its Match in AGB?" *Advertising Age* (October 7, 1985):4–93.

2. ———, "Nielsen Locks up Its Replacement for Diaries," *Advertising Age* (October 28, 1985):62.

3. Kevin T. Higgins, "Competition Intensifies as Nielsen, AGB Jockey for Audience Measurement Lead," *Marketing News* (November 22, 1985):1–6.

4. Barry M. Kaplan, "Zapping—The Real Issue Is Communication," *Journal of Advertising Research* (April/May 1985):9–12.

5. Kent M. Lancaster, Margaret A. Toomey, Sheryl A. Bahnks, and Sheri Kramer, *Advertising Media Plan Development and Evaluation,* working paper (Urbana: University of Illinois, 1985).

6. John Naisbitt, *Megatrends: Ten New Directions Transforming Our Lives* (New York: Warner Books, 1982).

7. Michael J. Naples, "Electronic Media Research: An Update and a Look at the Future," *Journal of Advertising Research* (August/September 1984):39–46.

8. David Owen, "Satellite Television," *Atlantic Monthly* (June 1985):45–62.

9. Rich Zahradnik, "Scrambling to Make TV Pay," *Channels* (July/August 1985):16–18.

10. Fred S. Zufryden, "A Tested Model of Purchase Response to Advertising Exposure," *Journal of Advertising Research* (February 1981):7–16.

Essential Media Models Terminology

ADSTAR A PC-based decision support system for media selection and evaluation.

Advertising media schedule A detailed schedule of when and where advertisements are placed.

Advertising medium The method of communication (such as television) in which an advertisement is used.

Audience flow model A model which describes and predicts television viewing based on how individuals change channels.

Average frequency The average number of exposures received by an individual, given that the individual was exposed.

Average issue audience The audience "rating" of a magazine. The proportion of the population exposed to a magazine.

Beta binomial distribution (BBD) A popular mathematical method for estimating the frequency distribution of exposure. Also known as the **Metheringham formula.**

Beta matrix method An ad hoc mathematical procedure for estimating the frequency distribution of exposure for a schedule with multiple insertions in each media vehicle.

Constraint In mathematical programming models, a condition which must be satisfied by the solution.

Cross-pair Two television programs (or, more generally, media vehicles) which are not episodes of the same program (or issues of the same magazine).

Decision support system (DSS) An integrated computer system which aids decision making, including communication programs, data bases, and computer models.

Direct broadcast satellite (DBS) Broadcasting television from a satellite to a relatively limited area, using a powerful broadcast signal and small satellite receiving dishes.

Dirichlet multinomial distribution (DMD) The multivariate analog of the beta binomial distribution. Used by some of the newer models to estimate the frequency distribution of exposure.

Duplication The audience shared by two (or more) media vehicles. Usually expressed as a proportion.

Duplication of Viewing Law The assertion that pairwise duplication is proportional to the product of the ratings of the various vehicles.

Dynamic programming A method of mathematical programming which utilizes recursive relationships.

Effective frequency The number of times (often assumed to be three) that an individual must be exposed to an advertisement before it is effective.

Evaluation model A model which assesses the likely response to a proposed schedule.

Exposure distribution See **frequency distribution of exposure.**

Flow state Television viewing state which reflects whether the television was previously on, whether it is tuned to the same channel as the viewing option under consideration, and whether or not the viewing option is a continuation of a program.

Frequency The number of times an individual is exposed to an advertising schedule. Sometimes used to indicate **average frequency.**

Frequency distribution of exposure The proportions of the population exposed to zero, one, two, etc. vehicles in the schedule. This gives more information than just reach and average frequency.

Gamma function A mathematical function needed to calculate frequency distributions using the beta binomial distribution.

Goal programming A method of mathematical programming which seeks a satisfactory solution rather than an optimal one.

Gross impressions (GIs) The sum of the average issue audiences in a magazine schedule.

Gross rating points (GRPs) The sum of the ratings in a television advertising schedule.

Heuristic model A model which uses a systematic search routine to find the solution, but does not guarantee global optimality.

Insertions Placements of advertisements in a particular media vehicle.

Integer programming A type of mathematical programming which generally requires a heuristic solution.

Intermedia duplication The (usually pairwise) duplication between media vehicles in different media (for example, television and magazine).

Joint frequency distribution of exposure A distribution which describes frequency of exposure to two or more media (or vehicles). In a television–magazine schedule, for example, the expression $f(2,3) = .1$ would mean that 10 percent of the population was exposed twice to television and three times to magazines.

Linear programming The simplest form of mathematical programming. Used for early media selection models.

Mathematical programming A mathematical technique in which an objective function is optimized subject to constraints.

Media selection model A model which chooses an optimal media schedule.

Media vehicle See **vehicle.**

MEDIAC Originally proposed in 1966, it was the first truly sophisticated media selection model, although the frequency distribution estimation procedure is now obsolete.

Medium See **advertising medium.**

Metheringham formula Another name for the beta binomial distribution method for estimating frequency distribution of exposure.

Mixed-media model A model which estimates the joint frequency distribution of exposure for a schedule involving two or more media.

MRI Mediamark. A syndicated data service which provides magazine audience data and other media data.

Nielsen (A.C. Nielsen Company) The most widely used source in the United States for television viewing data.

Objective function A mathematical expression for sales, profit, or some other quantity which is to be optimized in a mathematical program.

Pairwise duplication The duplicated audience of two media vehicles.

Pay per view (PPV) A cable television technology by which households may pay specifically for particular programs.

Program scheduling model A model which finds the optimal time slots for an inventory of programs, from the point of view of a television network.

Program type A classification summarizing the content of a program (for example, comedy).

Rating The proportion of the population viewing a particular television program. Often expresssed in whole numbers as a percentage.

Reach The proportion of the population which is exposed at least once to a vehicle or schedule.

Response function A mathematical function which expresses the expected response for each possible number of exposures to a schedule.

Satellite television (STV) A broadcast technology by which large satellite dishes are used to pick up the weak broadcast signals emitted by communications satellites.

Schedule See **advertising media schedule.**

Self-pair A pair of insertions in the same vehicle (such as two episodes of "Miami Vice").

Simulation model A model which uses random probabilities to evaluate or select media schedules.

SMRB Formerly Simmons, the leading United States supplier of magazine readership data.

Two-way cable A cable technology by which the television viewer may send communications back across the cable to select programs, etc.

Vehicle A specific television program, magazine, etc. on which to advertise.

Videocassette Recorder (VCR) A video tape recorder which uses cassettes for storage.

Zapping Skipping over a commercial via a remote control device or fast-forward VCR control.

Index

Subject Index

Author Index

About the Author

Roland T. Rust is associate professor of marketing administration at the University of Texas at Austin. He holds a Ph.D. and an M.B.A. in business administration from the University of North Carolina at Chapel Hill, and a B.A. in mathematics from DePauw University. He has published widely in the fields of advertising media planning and research methodology in such journals as *Marketing Science, Journal of Marketing Research, Journal of Marketing,* and *Journal of Advertising.* He is a member of the *Journal of Marketing Research* editorial review board. He is active in The American Academy of Advertising, The American Statistical Association, and The Institute of Management Sciences.

He is currently working (with Mark Alpert) under a grant from the Marketing Science Institute, supported by ABC, CBS, and MSI, to study television viewing choice in a cable environment.